PAUL HENDERSON SCOTT was born in Edinburgh and educated at the Royal High School and Edinburgh University. He was in 52nd (Lowland) and 7th Armed Divisions during the war and then joined the Diplomatic Service. He was in Berlin during the whole of the Soviet blockade and in Cuba during the Missile Crisis. In 1980 he returned to Edinburgh. Since then he has been Rector of Dundee University, President of both the Saltire Society and Scottish PEN, and Vice-President of the SNP and its Spokesman on Culture and International Affairs as well as writing more than a dozen books and editing another dozen or so. His books include: *Walter Scott and Scotland, John Galt, Towards Independence, Andrew Fletcher and the Treaty of Union, Still in Bed with an Elephant, Defoe in Edinburgh and Other Papers, The Boasted Advantages, A 20th Century Life* (his autobiography*), Scotland Resurgent, The Union of 1707: Why and How, The Age of Liberation* and *The New Scotland*.

HARRY REID was born in Glasgow and educated in Aberdeen, Edinburgh and Oxford. He trained to be a journalist in Newcastle and then worked in the Scottish Press for 33 years, mainly on the *Scotsman* and the *Herald*, of which he was Editor. In 2001 he was awarded honorary doctorates by Edinburgh and Glasgow Universities for his services to Scottish journalism. He is a former chairman of the Scottish Editors' Committee. He has written a bestselling study of the Church of Scotland and three other books including his recent history of the European Reformation. His wife is the travel writer Julie Davidson.

STEPHEN MAXWELL was born in Edinburgh in 1942 into a Scottish medical family. He grew up and was educated in Yorkshire before winning a scholarship to St John's College Cambridge where he read Moral Sciences followed by three years at the London School of Economics studying International Politics. Attracted by the stirring of Scottish Nationalism in the mid '60s he joined the London branch of the SNP in 1967. He worked as a research associate of the International Institute for Strategic Studies in London and a Lecturer in International Affairs at the University of Sussex before returning to Scotland as Chatham House Research Fellow at the University of Edinburgh in 1970. He was a frequent contributor to the cultural and political journals from *Scottish International Review* through *Question to Radical Scotland* which fertilised the Scottish debate from the 1970s to the 1990s. From 1973 to 78 he was the SNP's National Press Officer and was director of the SNP's campaign in the 1979 Scottish Assembly Referendum. He was a SNP Councillor on Lothian Regional Council 1975–78 before serving as an SNP Vice Chair for successively Publicity, Policy and Local Government. From the mid 1980s he worked in the voluntary sector first with Scottish Education and Action for Development (SEAD), and then for the Scottish Council for Voluntary Organisations (SCVO) until he retired in 2009. He was the founding chair of a Scottish charitable company which today provides support to six hundred vulnerable people to live in the community. He has contributed to numerous collections of essays on Scotland's future, most recently *The Modern SNP: from protest to power* (ed Hassan, FUP 2009) and *Nation in A State* (ed Brown, Ten Book Press 2007). He is Treasurer of the Scottish Independence Convention.

TOM NAIRN, after serving time on the hulk of HMS Britain, escaped to teaching 'Nationalism Studies' at Edinburgh University, then to researching 'Globalisation and Nationalism' at the Royal Melbourne Institute of Technology in Victoria, Australia. His book *The Break-up of Britain* appeared in 1977 (Verso Books, most recent edition Common Ground Publishing, Melbourne, 2003). *Faces of Nationalism* (Verso) appeared in 1997 and *Global Matrix* (Pluto Press, with Paul James) in 2005.

NEIL KAY has Bachelors and Doctorate degrees from Stirling and is Professor (Emeritus) Economics Dept., University of Strathclyde; Special Professor in the Business School, University of Nottingham; and was Visiting Professor Economics Department, University of Queensland, Australia, 2005, 2006 and 2007. He has also held two Visiting Associate Professorships in the University of California and a part-time Professorship in the Economics Department in the EC's official university in Florence. He is author of six books and numerous articles on industrial economics and the economics of corporate strategies. He lives in Cowal, Argyll with his wife Lorna and two children, Katerina and Kieran.

BETTY DAVIES was born in Nottinghamshire. She graduated from the Guildhall School of Music and Drama in the '60s and worked for a short time in television and the theatre. In 1993, together with the late Douglas Henderson, one of the driving forces for Scottish independence and SNP MP for East Aberdeenshire, she founded the successful design and management organisation Scottish Fashion International, branding the major Scottish banks and financial service sector with distinctive tartans and classic outfits. Her dramatic hallmark for ceremonial dress now adds gravitas and colour to many of Scotland's important academic and state occasions. Active in the public and private sector, she has continued to work in England and Scotland where she has served as a Magistrate, a public member of the Press Council, and a Member of Court of Nottingham University. A former Governor of Edinburgh College of Art, in 2004 she was made an Honorary Fellow for her contribution to the visual and performing arts. From her lofty studio in the Old Town of Edinburgh her work in the field of art and communication continues. During most her lifetime Betty Davies has remained mute on her political allegiance. This contribution to *A National Again* celebrates the life of the late Douglas Henderson and the legacy of a courageous and proud people.

Viewpoints is an occasional series exploring issues of current and future relevance.

Luath Press is an independently owned and managed book publishing company based in Scotland, and is not aligned to any political party or grouping.

A Nation Again

Why Independence will be good for Scotland
(and England too)

Edited by

PAUL HENDERSON SCOTT

With contributions by the Editor and

HARRY REID, STEPHEN MAXWELL, TOM NAIRN,
NEIL KAY and BETTY DAVIES

Luath Press Limited

EDINBURGH

www.luath.co.uk

First published 2008
(as *The Independence Book*)
Reprinted 2008
Reprinted 2009
Revised and extended edition 2011

ISBN: 978-1-906817-67-1

The paper used in this book is recyclable. It is made from low chlorine pulps
produced in a low energy, low emission manner from renewable forests.

Printed and bound by
Bell & Bain Ltd., Glasgow

Typeset in 11.5 point Sabon by
3btype.com

Contents

Foreword

I AM DELIGHTED to write a Foreword for the new edition of this book which is an important contribution to the debate about the future of Scotland.

This is a collective book by six people with a wide range of experience. The editor, Paul Henderson Scott, was born and educated in Edinburgh, and has a wide experience of other countries as a diplomat. Since he returned to Edinburgh in 1980 he has been active in many aspects of Scottish life. He has been Rector of Dundee University, President of the Saltire Society and of Scottish PEN, Vice-President of the SNP and a Spokesman on culture and international affairs. He has written 17 books, mostly about Scottish history, politics and literature and has edited or contributed to many others.

In this book there are papers by the editor and others by five distinguished contributors. Harry Reid has worked for Scottish newspapers, including the editorship of *The Herald*, for 33 years. He has written several books, of which the latest is a study of the Reformation which ranges widely over European history. Stephen Maxwell, who was National Press Officer of the SNP from 1973 to 1978, is a frequent contributor to cultural and political journals and to books of collected essays on Scotland's future. Tom Nairn has been a major stimulator of thought and debate about the constitutional future of Scotland to which many people were introduced by his brilliant book, The *Break-Up of Britain*. Neil Kay has been a professor of economics in England, Australia, the USA and Italy. Betty Davies has had a highly successful career in Scotland as a fashion designer and producer. She was a partner for many years of the late Douglas Henderson who was an SNP MP. Her long experience of life in Scotland has convinced her that Scottish independence would be of great benefit to both Scotland and England.

The significance of this book is that these highly informed and intelligent people with very diverse experience have all reached that same conclusion. We have a great past as a nation which has made a valuable contribution to the world. At a time when many other smaller European countries have flourished since they recovered independence, we urgently need to follow their example. We need full responsibility for the control of our own affairs and of our relationship with the rest of the world.

Alex Salmond,
First Minister of Scotland

Reekie, 2000
Paul Henderson Scott

For Dunbar it was the mirry toun.
Fergusson cried it a canty hole
And like a keek o glore and heaven forby
Here Hume transformed human thocht
And gave bien denners tae his freens.
Clerk Maxwell as a bairn at schule
Scrievit a paper for the Royal Society.

For thae that hae the lugs tae hear
Thae splores, high jinks, high thochts
Sill echo roon closes, wynds,
Howfs and new toun drawing rooms.
In oor ain time Garioch and Smith
Were guy sib to Fergusson himsel.
The sheer beauty o the place still lifts the hert,
A beauty which some hae done their best tae hash

For there's muckle to gar ye grue
In Auld Reikie and in aw Scotland thae days:
Puirtith, ignorance and hopelessness,
Shoddy bigins, ill health, early daith,
Amang the warst in Europe tae oor shame.
Cheek by jowl wi commercial greed,
Affluence, mobile phones and jaunts tae Bangkok,
Efter three hunner year o nae government or misgovernment.

But noo there's a glisk o hope.
At last we hae oor Parliament back,
Reined yet by Westminster,
But sune we'll ding thae traces doon.
Ower lang oor caws for equality and social justice
Hae fallen on deif and distant lugs.
Sune we shall bigg a new and fairer Scotland
Wi Reikie a real capital aince mair.

Introduction

THE AUTHORS, five men and one woman, of the six essays in this book are not exactly in the first flush of youth. Indeed they have a collective age of over 350. They are respected figures who have achieved considerable success in their own fields. They also have wide experience of not least because of their enthusiasm for Scottish independence.

Their voices are individual and distinctive, and their perspectives are very different. But they are bound together by one essential denominator – their total commitment to the imperative of independence. That is their common cause.

Once that great goal is achieved, they well understand that it is not they who will benefit: it will be the young people of Scotland. It will be for the young people of Scotland to make a free Scotland a long-term working reality. It will be for the young people of Scotland to mould a bright and better future for their own children and grandchildren, and all the generations to come. But first we need to achieve independence.

The case for independence is what this book is all about. It is imbued with urgency and enthusiasm. But it is most definitely NOT about what precisely would happen in an independent Scotland, because nobody knows. That is the whole point. The people of Scotland would at long last be empowered to decide what their country was to be like and the direction it was to take. At the beginning, there would be an open book. So it is not the purpose of this book to discuss exactly what an independent Scotland would and would not do.

Those who are now youngsters in today's Scotland will be resolving such matters and questions in the years to come. The authors of this book are fully aware that the blossoming of an independent Scotland will be a long process. They will not live to see all the fruits of the confidence, the empowering, the freedom. But that does not stop their fervent wish to achieve for Scots in the centuries to come this grandest and most exciting of opportunities. For what can be more exciting than a nation starting afresh, and getting the chance to fulfil its aspirations, dreams and visions?

It is however more than an opportunity, however grand. It is also a responsibility. Moulding the future is work that is challenging and responsible as well as heady and invigorating.

History will be made, not just in the achievement of independence, but in all the months and years ahead as the new state rolls out its policies and its programmes.

There is no naïve suggestion in this book that an independent Scotland would be operating in some benign vacuum. No modern nation state can be truly, purely independent in a world that is predicated on interdependency as never before. Transnational institutions have enormous importance. It is folly to claim that any nation-state can operate in glorious isolation.

But then that is not the sort of claim our six authors make. They are rather writing about something that is honourable and just; the need for a nation, a proud and historic nation, to fulfil its potential as a state as well. It is wrong that a nation like Scotland, known the world over, should have been subsumed for so long into a much larger state. Scotland, at present, finds itself in the sad limbo of stateless nationhood.

The other crucial point for readers to note is that this book is in no way infused with anti-English sentiment. Far from it. Each of the authors, in their various distinctive ways, believes that an independent Scotland would actually be good for England. Each of them sincerely wishes England well.

Meanwhile the first great step, at once simple, historic and momentous, has to be taken, and that is to achieve independence. This book is about that inescapable imperative.

CHAPTER I

Independence is the Answer

PAUL HENDERSON SCOTT

IN HIS CELEBRATED BOOK, *Small is Beautiful,* E. F. Schumacher challenged the theory in which he had been brought up. That was the belief that 'in order to be prosperous a country had to be big – the bigger the better'. On the contrary he found that 'if we make a list of all the most prosperous countries in the world, we find that most of them are very small; whereas a list of the biggest countries in the world shows most of them to be very poor indeed... In the actual world there is a tremendous longing and striving to profit, if at all possible, from the convenience, humanity and manageability of smallness'[1].

Schumacher's point is confirmed by the latest available statistics for the countries of the European Union. They show that the six most prosperous are small:-

	GDP per head (in purchasing power standard)	Population (in millions)
Luxembourg	58,900	0.5
Ireland	32,600	4.2
Netherlands	29,500	16.3
Austria	28,900	8.3
Denmark	28,600	5.4
Belgium	27,700	10.5

They are followed by the UK with a GDP per head of 27,600 and a population of 60.4 million; but Luxembourg the smallest is also by far the most prosperous[2].

Long before Schumacher, others had reached the same conclusion, including two of the key figures of the Scottish Enlightenment. David

Hume in his essay, *Idea of a Perfect Commonwealth* said: 'A small commonwealth is the happiest government in the world, within itself, because everything lies under the eye of the rulers'[3]. Adam Ferguson in *An Essay on the History of Civil Society* of 1767, wrote of the advantages of living in society and added:

> We need not enlarge our communities in order to enjoy these advantages. We frequently obtain them the most remarkable degree, where nations remain independent, and are of small extent[4].

Both Hume and Ferguson were, of course, writing only a few decades after Scotland had lost her independence in the Union of 1707.

In recent years, particularly since the end of World War II, there has been a rapid increase in the number of small states. The present is the Age of Liberation (the title of my recent book) in which nearly all of the multi-national states and the empires have dissolved into their component parts. When Schumacher published *Small is Beautiful* in 1947 he said 'The United Nations Organisation started some 25 years ago with some 60 members; now there are more than twice as many, and the number is still growing'[5]. Following the recent successful referendum on independence in Southern Sudan, the number of member states will soon reach 193.

As it happens, I have been able to witness the progress which has been achieved by two of these new states since they became independent. I have been lecturing on cruises to the Baltic and have visited Estonia several times. Slovenian PEN holds an annual conference of writers which is so interesting, welcoming and friendly that participation each year has become an addiction. The change in both of these countries since they became independent has been dramatic. Not only have they become rapidly much more prosperous, but also unmistakably more self-confident, optimistic and quite simply happier.

The Scottish Enlightenment invented the idea, which was later adopted in the American Declaration of Independence, that the object of government is the pursuit of happiness. Estonia and Slovenia have demonstrated it in practice. In my years as a diplomat I visited many countries and I have always had the impression that small countries were happier than the large. It is probably because the smaller are more homogeneous and their governments are closer to the people and have an easier task in meeting their wishes and needs. Norway is a small country which became independent from Sweden just over a century ago and is now one of the most prosperous and contented in the world. A Norwegian professor at the University of Oslo, Johan P. Olsen, has said the following of the advantages of the small states:

> Many smaller European states have a good historical record when it comes to democratic development, peaceful co-existence, prosperity, welfare, equality between social classes, districts and gender, life expectancy, cultural development and ecological consciousness. A democratic argument has been that the political community has to be small in order for citizens to have insight, participation, influence and a feeling of belonging and trust.

He adds that in this globalised world small states have more experience than the larger of coping with events over which they have no control and are therefore better in responding to them[6].

In his contribution to this book Tom Nairn also discusses the advantages which small nations have in responding to the challenges of a globalised world. They also benefit from the increased role of international organisations such as the United Nations and the European Union. Their effect is to curb the power of the large countries and increase the influence of the small. Several heads of government of the smaller members of the European Union have made this point. For instance Poul Schlüter, when he was Prime Minister of Denmark, said:

> I feel a lot more powerful than a Danish Prime Minister would have felt years ago. Why? Because under all circumstances this is a rather small neighbouring country to Germany and the strong economy. In the old days, we just had to accept any

steps taken in the German economy, and its consequences on us. Nowadays, my ministers and I take part in the Council of Ministers meetings in Europe. We have influence, and a lot more influence than is fair, considering that we are such a small nation[7].

Garret Fitzgerald, a former Prime Minister of Ireland, in a speech in 1989:

Over a period of many years, I have come to the paradoxical conclusion that it is in the process of merging its sovereignty with other Member States in the Community that Ireland has found the clearest 'ex post facto' justification for its long struggle to achieve independence from the United Kingdom[8].

Mary Robinson, when she was President of Ireland, said in a speech when she was on a visit to Scotland in June 1992:

There has been a great sense of liberation. We have become more sure of our own Irish identity in the context of being equal partners in Europe. It meant that we no longer simply define ourselves in terms of our relationship with Britain.

We are Irish but we are also European… Ireland and Scotland have much in common yet there are very few institutional links that recognise this. We must build them up[9].

The Disadvantages of the Union

The historian, Hume Brown said of the Union of the Crowns of 1603, when James VI of Scotland became also James I of England:

The Union of the crowns brought many disadvantages to Scotland, but the result of it that most vitally affected her was her severance from the nations at a period when new principles and new ideas were guiding their policy.

> Throughout the entire century Scotland was a severed and withered branch, and her people knew it[10].

This was a time when the existence of a nation and the conduct of its foreign policy were closely identified with the monarch. The countries of Europe, which were accustomed to dealing with an independent Scotland, now had the impression that it had been absorbed by England. This view was confirmed by the parliamentary union of 1707. The English Parliament was to continue as before, except only for the addition of very few Scottish members. In the Commons of 558 members Scotland was to have 45, only one more than the county of Cornwall. In the Lords there would be only 16 Scottish peers, although the Church of England alone had 26 bishops. It is not surprising that the rest of Europe refused to be deceived by the adoption of the new term, Britain. Even our oldest ally, France, stuck like the others to their word for England. That was a recognition of the reality.

A small country in a union with a larger one, such as Scotland with England, is always at a disadvantage. Inevitably the larger country is likely to put its own interests first, and react to the ideas and attitudes of their own people, in preference to those of the smaller. In fact, it could be said that this is democratically proper because the views of the majority should prevail. Scotland is a country which evolved over centuries of independent history. For much of this time Scotland was in much closer contact, politically, culturally and intellectually, with other countries in Europe than with England. Even after the Union the church, the law, education, literature and music remained distinct from those of England. It is therefore not surprising that Scottish ideas and aspirations, politically and culturally are often very different from those of England.

An important example of this is in attitudes to international affairs. The majority view in England evidently is that the country should still aspire to the role of a great power. It is presumably for this reason that the UK Government clings to nuclear weapons and regards itself as the major ally of the United States. In fact, that makes it more of a puppet than a partner. This has led to British involvement in the illegal and disastrous Iraq war and the encouragement of terrorism. The majority of Scots are opposed to nuclear weapons and would prefer to see Scotland playing a co-operative, rational and peaceful role in the world.

Some opponents of Scottish independence are given to asking in an incredulous tone, as if it was self-evidently absurd, 'a Scottish diplomatic service, army, navy and airforce?' Of course, many countries in Europe which are smaller than Scotland, maintain all of these things of a scale and nature which are perfectly adequate for their needs. An independent Scotland could easily do the same. They would cost less than the contribution which Scotland makes through UK taxation to inflated ideas of Britain's role in the world. These forces would be appropriate to our needs and, like our own diplomatic service, would not be distracted by other objectives.

Many Scots are astonished and exasperated by the way some people in England cling to this absurd notion of the country as still a great and imperial power free from the restraints of international organisations. The novelist Iain Banks expressed this in an interview with the *Edinburgh Evening News*:

> I'm at the stage of thinking we have to leave England to its fate. If it wants to leave the EU, then let it stew in its own past imperial dreamland. Scotland can be a great small country in Europe. We can make a success of it and be a more humane society than this privatised and selfishness oriented country[11].

Nuclear Submarines

The British Government has not only insisted on retaining and renewing nuclear-armed submarines, but on stationing them on the Clyde, close to our largest centre of population. This is a violation of obligations under the treaty against the proliferation of nuclear weapons and tends to encourage other countries to follow this bad example. They present a permanent risk of a catastrophic accident or terrorist attack. They are not, as they are described, an 'independent deterrent' because they are dependent on American co-operation. Also they serve no real purpose. At the time of the Cold War, the submarines cruised with their nuclear weapons targeted at sites in the Soviet Union. Where are they targeted now? The official estimate of the cost of renewing these submarines is £15 to 20 billion. Other estimates are even higher. As long as the Union continues, about a tenth of this would fall on the Scottish taxpayer. If we deny the use of the Clyde base, either through ending the Union or in some other interim way, it would be difficult to find an English constituency that would be prepared to tolerate the submarines on their doorstep. If that were to lead to the abandonment of the whole project that would be of benefit to us all.

Scottish Oil

Another very obvious disadvantage of the Union is the assumption, or seizure, by the British Government of the revenue from the oil in Scottish waters.

When the oil was discovered in the 1970s a senior Treasury official said in a memorandum to ministers:

> It is conceivable that income per head in Scotland could be 25 per cent or 30 per cent higher than that prevailing in England during the 1980s, given independence[12].

Since this was obviously a strong argument for Scottish independence ministers of both Conservative and Labour Governments did their best to confuse the issue by concealing the great potential value of the oil reserves. In fact their value in the last six years alone has been £38 billion and the official estimate is that it will be about £55 billion over the next five or six years. With such wealth under the control of an independent Scotland, we could, like Norway, build up a reserve fund to guarantee our prosperity for the indefinite future. And, of course, this is an asset which has grown enormously in value with the steady increase in the price of oil.

The Need for Scottish Membership of the European Union

Another major disadvantage of the Union is that it denies Scotland our own membership of the international organisations, especially the European Union. British representatives to it generally ignore Scottish interests or views when they differ from those of England. The senior Scottish official in our European office, Michael Avon, made this very clear in a letter to the then Labour First Minister, Jack McConnell in September 2006. He complained that Whitehall officials normally ignore Scottish views. Whitehall, he said, 'appeared to be under the impression that their policy views and objectives were representative of the entire UK, rather than those of England'[13]. This was particularly unfortunate in matters of fishing policy. Scotland had more than 70 per cent of the UK fishing fleet and 90 per cent of its fish farming. British representatives in Brussels have constantly sacrificed the interests of Scottish fishing for the sake of some other advantage. An industry which is important to Scotland, but not to anything like the same extent to England, has been devastated in consequence.

Scottish independence does not mean separation, as the Labour Party frequently alleges. Gordon Brown, for example, in his speech to the Scottish Labour Party conference on 28 March 2008 said: 'This is an interdependent world. What sense would it make within these islands to separate Scotland from the rest of Britain and make it more difficult to travel and trade? The Union enhances the influence of Scottish people and ideas'[14]. Brown is living in the past when the world was dominated by the empires and the multi-national states. Almost all of them have now dissolved into their component parts. Because of this, and the increased role of international organisations, the world has become much more interdependent. Scotland can only benefit from it when we join the modern world by recovering independence.

An independent Scotland would remain a member of the European Union and a valuable one because of our skilled population and resources including oil and fish. Our freedom of movement and trade is not confined to Britain, as Brown seems to suggest, but includes the whole area of the European Union and much of the rest of the world. Scotland can become a full and active participant in the new interdependent world as a member state of the EU and the UN. Another Labour Minister, Des Browne, had the habit of attaching the adjective 'parochial' to the aspirations of the SNP Government whenever he mentions it, as he did at the same conference[15]. For centuries the Scots have been enthusiastic cosmopolitans. The parochial are those who want to deny us our right to participate in the world at large.

Opponents of Scottish independence have suggested that Scotland would not automatically remain a member of the European Union when it achieves independence, and would have to apply as a new applicant. There are no grounds in European legislation for this opinion. Several senior authorities have confirmed this. For instance, Emile Noel, a former Secretary General of the European Commission, said:

> There is no precedent and no provision for the expulsion of a member state, therefore Scottish independence would create two new member states out of one. They would have equal status with each other and with the other member states.
>
> The remainder of the United Kingdom would not be in a more powerful position than Scotland. ... Anyone attacking the claim in respect of one country is attacking it in respect of the other. It's not possible to divide the cases[16].

Both countries would have to negotiate such matters as their voting strength in the Council and number of members in the European Parliament. Since there would be no need for a new application, there would be no risk of a suspension of membership or of a veto.

The Psychological Damage Inflicted by the Union

It is not in economic matters alone that Scotland suffers from the Union. The psychological consequences in the loss of self-knowledge and self-confidence is even more damaging. That this can be said of the Scots of all peoples is extraordinary. For centuries before the Union Scotland played an active and constructive part in European affairs. Scots studied and taught in European universities. Between its foundation and the Reformation 17 or 18 of the Rectors of the University of Paris were Scots[17]. In the 17th century George Buchanan was celebrated all over Europe as the best poet in Latin since classical times. Several Scots served European governments as ministers and diplomats, a rare act of confidence in foreigners. Scots were in demand to assist in the development of many countries. Lord Macaulay attributed this to the quality of Scottish education, and he was of course speaking of Scottish education in the 16th and 17th centuries:

> It began to be evident that the common people of Scotland were superior in intelligence to the common people of any country in Europe... Scotland made good progress in all that constitutes civilisation... This wonderful change is to be attributed, not indeed solely, but principally to the national system of education[18].

Following the discovery of America and the rest of the world Scots made an important contribution to the development of many countries overseas, particularly, but not confined to, North America and the Empire.

Inside Scotland itself our history has been one of remarkable achievement. For three centuries we successfully survived attacks by our larger and more powerful neighbour. In the course of this we evolved ideas of equality and representative government. Many Americans regard the Declaration of Arbroath of 1320 as the source from which their own constitution derives. The Church of Scotland created a democratic structure for the control of its affairs centuries before any parliament did the same. In ideas, scientific discovery, exploration, literature and the arts Scotland has a remarkable record. In the words of the American, Harold Orel in his book on Scotland, 'no nation of its size has contributed as much to world culture'[19]. And, of course, another American, Arthur Herman, in his book, *The Scottish Enlightenment: The Scots' Invention of the Modern World* concluded : 'As the first modern nation and culture, the Scots have by and large made the world a better place'[20].

The obvious question is how can the people of such a country possibly lack self-confidence? The immediate answer is that a great many Scots, probably the majority, know virtually nothing about the history and literature of their own country. This is, of course, shocking and disgraceful, especially in a country with a past of such rich achievement as Scotland. As the English historian, J. A. Froude said: 'No nation in Europe can look back with more just pride on their past than the Scots, and no young Scot ought to grow up in ignorance of what that past has been'[21]. But that is precisely what has happened. For several generations our schools have largely ignored our own history and literature, and so have the broadcasters, to an extent probably unique in the developed world. Our children have been given the impression that they are growing up in a backward and benighted place which has never accomplished anything of importance. It is not surprising that many want to leave as soon as they can.

This has been a consequence, slowly but probably inevitably, of the Union of 1707, a process which is the subject of Michael Hechter's book, *Internal Colonialism*, published in 1975. He concludes that in order to assert authority the centre 'must disparage the indigenous culture of peripheral groups'. It does this by claiming its own culture is 'vastly superior' for the realisation of universal ends. This 'process of anglicisation' is carried through 'not only by government fiat, but through the voluntary assimilation of peripheral elites'[22]. That such a process has been carried through and is still in action is, I think, undeniable; but it has probably been more unconscious than deliberate.

It is the natural consequence of a Union in which one partner is so much larger and wealthier than the other and has all the instruments of power in its control.

This process has been helped too by the self-confidence of the English and their assumption that they enjoy a natural superiority over the rest of us. The 'peripheral elite', as Hechter calls it, from Scotland, who sought royal patronage, or political or worldly success in London, had to play by these rules. Schools in Scotland began to feel obliged to assist in this process. The bairns could only succeed in the world if they learnt to speak English. The consequences of this gradually spread through Scotland. In Derrick McClure's words, 'In the 19th century, even the name and identity of Scotland, and every-thing that made it distinctively Scottish, became suspect as the Scots came to regard English mores, as the English themselves regarded them – as the natural models for the rest of the world'[23].

The undermining of Scottish self-confidence began effectively in the 19th century because that was when the British Empire dominated Scottish life. Many Scots made brilliant careers in its administration and millions emigrated to it. Others opened up new territories through exploration. Scottish regiments in a more controversial role were active in its expansion and security. Scottish industry built a major part of the ships and railway locomotives which served it. Other Scottish industries imported raw materials from it and exported their products to it. All of this was, as Linda Colley has said, 'a British imperium... The English and the foreign are still all too inclined today to refer to the island of Great Britain as 'England'. But at no time have they ever referred to an *English* empire'[24]. Since this institution had become so important in the life of Scotland and since Scotland was a partner in it only because of the Union, there was pressure towards Scottish opinion taking a favourable view of the Union itself.

Distortions in Unionist Propaganda

It was in this atmosphere that two theories about the Union began to be accepted which place it in a favourable light, but which are in fact false. They have survived to the present and probably colour the attitude of many people to the Union and therefore to Scottish independence. They have become so thoroughly established that even reputable academics still to this day repeat them as if they were undeniable truths. Since they have survived so long and with so much effect, it is, I think, appropriate to explain them in some detail.

The first of these is a version of the origin of the Union. It is said that the failure of the Darien scheme imposed such a loss on Scotland that the Scottish Parliament had to seek the help of the English. In response the English Government proposed negotiations. These led to a Treaty which was freely negotiated and ratified by the Scottish Parliament. It included the full compensation by the British Government of the losses of the Darien investors and access to Scottish traders to the English colonial markets. The two countries were merged into one, called Great Britain, with a combined Parliament. Scotland prospered accordingly.

It all sounds too good to be true, and that is what it is. All of these statements are the precise opposite of the truth. After Darien the Scottish Parliament did not seek English help; but in the sessions of 1703 and 1704 voted repeatedly for the recovery of Scottish independence and the restoration of a separate Scottish monarchy. Godolphin, the leading minister in the English Government, in a letter to Seafield, the Scottish Chancellor, threatened war. The English Parliament then passed an Act proposing negotiations, but also threatening stringent economic sanctions if the Scots did not accept the same succession to the throne as England by 25 December 1705. When the Scottish Parliament discussed the appointment of commissioners for negotiations in London, Hamilton (almost certainly because of bribery) contrived a decision that this should be left to the Queen. This meant that both teams of negotiators were appointed by the English Government and a genuine and free negotiation was therefore impossible.

The Treaty of Union which emerged provided for the abolition of the Scottish Parliament, and for Scottish access to trade with the English colonies. It also imposed heavy financial burdens on Scotland in the

form of a share in liability for the English National Debt and the impo-
sition of English excise duties. In compensation for these, and to repay
the losses of the Scottish investors in Darien, a sum of money, called
the Equivalent, was to be paid to Scotland. In fact, this sum was inade-
quate to cover all its purposes and even that amount was never paid
in full. In a debate which lasted from October 1706 to January 1707
the Scottish Parliament approved the Treaty. This was the same Parliament with the same members who had voted repeatedly in favour of
Scottish independence. There is little room for doubt that they yielded
to bribery and the threat of invasion. The population at large protested
against the Union by demonstrations in the streets and a flood of
addresses, all against and not one in favour. The Parliament, like all
others at that time, was completely unrepresentative, consisting only
of lords, lairds and members provided by the oligarchies that controlled the burghs.

The immediate effect of the Treaty was to depress the Scottish
economy for several decades. Adam Smith in a letter in 1760
explained the reasons:

> The immediate effect of it was to hurt the interest of every
> single order of men in the country... Even the merchants
> seemed to suffer at first. The trade to the Plantations was,
> indeed, opened to them. But that was a trade which they knew
> nothing about; the trade they were acquainted with, that to
> France, Holland and the Baltic, was laid under new embarrass-
> ments which almost totally annihilated the two first and most
> important branches... No wonder if at that time all orders of
> men conspired in cursing a measure so hurtful to their imme-
> diate interest.[25]

The other long-enduring myth is the allegation, often repeated even by
serious historians of literature, that Walter Scott was an enthusiast
for the Union. In the present climate, his views on such a matter may
seem unimportant; but his significance in his own lifetime and for at
least a century afterwards was as dominant as his monument in

Edinburgh suggests. He was regarded not only as one of the greatest Scottish writers but as a great Scottish patriot who had restored the self-confidence of the Scottish people and their awareness of their own history. When Scott died in 1832 Henry Cockburn said of him in his Journal: 'Scotland never owed so much to one man'[26]. Harold Macmillan in an address to the Edinburgh Sir Walter Scott Club said: 'For Scotland, he achieved two great ends. He made her people and her history known in every part of the civilised world. In addition he made Scotland known to herself'[27].

Clearly if such a man approved of the Union, who could be against it? But again, the facts are quite different. Throughout his life Scott was deeply worried that the effect of the Union would be to destroy the distinctive character of Scotland. Lockhart in his *Life of Scott* describes an episode in 1806 when Scott had been at a meeting in the Faculty of Advocates at which changes in legal procedure were discussed. As he walked down the Mound afterwards with some of his fellow advocates, Francis Jeffrey congratulated Scott on his eloquence and energy in opposing the changes and treated the matter playfully. Lockhart continues:

> But his feelings had been moved to an extent far beyond their apprehension: he exclaimed: 'No, No 'tis no laughing matter; little by little, whatever your wishes may be, you will destroy and undermine, until nothing that makes Scotland Scotland shall remain.'
>
> And so saying, he turned round to conceal his agitation – but not until Mr Jeffrey saw tears gushing down his cheek – resting his head until he recovered himself on the wall of the Mound[28].

In his *Tales of a Grandfather*, a history of Scotland for children, Scott wrote a frank account of the way in which England had achieved the Union. He concluded:

> Men of whom a majority had thus been bought and sold, forfeited every right to interfere in the terms which England

insisted upon... but despised by the English, and detested by
their own country, ... had no alternative left save that of
fulfilling the unworthy bargain they had made... a total sur-
render of their independence, by their false and corrupted
statesmen into the hand of their proud and powerful rival[29].

Angus Calder has a point when he says that it was possible in the late
18th century even for Walter Scott to tolerate the Union because 'so
far, it had not entailed any serious loss of Scottish distinctiveness
imposed by England'[30]. Earlier in the century the British Parliament
had seriously intervened in Scottish affairs by passing an Act providing
for the appointment of ministers in the Church of Scotland by landowners and not by election by the congregation. Eventually this led
to the division of the Church by the Disruption of 1843. In the middle
of the 18th century the British Government defeated, with Scottish
participation, the Jacobite rising and then proceeded to destroy the
established form of Highland society. Even so, it is true that the
British Government for the rest of the century, having reduced Scotland
to political impotence, generally left it to find its own way with its
remaining institutions.

This began to change early in the 19th century to the alarm of
Walter Scott. He seized the opportunity presented by the Government's proposal in 1826 of an Act to abolish the right of Scottish
banks to issue their own bank notes He said in a letter to his close
associate, John Ballantyne: 'I shall sleep quieter in my grave for having
so fair an opportunity of speaking my mind'[31]. This he did in three
strongly worded essays in an Edinburgh newspaper which were subsequently published as a pamphlet, *The Letters of Malachi Malagrowther on the Proposed Change of Currency*. They are the first mani-
festo of modern Scottish nationalism.

Scotland, he said, 'was left from the year 1750 under the
guardianship of her own institutions, to find her silent way to national
wealth and consequence'. This she had achieved with such success that
she:

has increased her prosperity in a ratio more than five times greater than that of her more fortunate and richer sister. She is now worth the attention of the learned faculty, and God knows she has had plenty of it... A spirit of proselytism has of late shown itself in England for extending the benefits of their system, in all its strengths and weaknesses, to a country, which has hitherto flourishing and contented under its own. They adopted the conclusion, that all English enactments are right; but the system of municipal law in Scotland is not English, therefore it is wrong... There has been in England a gradual and progressive system of assuming the management of affairs entirely and exclusively proper to Scotland, as if we were totally unworthy of having the management of our own concerns. All must centre in London... Good Heaven, sir! To what are we fallen? – or rather, what are we esteemed by the English? Wretched drivellers, incapable of understanding our own affairs; or greedy peculators, unfit to be trusted? On what ground are we considered either the one or the other?... For God's sake, sir, let us remain as Nature made us. Englishmen, Irishmen and Scotchmen, with something like the impress of our several countries upon each!... The Scottish Members of Parliament should therefore lose no time – not an instant – in uniting together in their national character of the Representatives of Scotland[32].

Scott's indignation, and his worry for the future, were clearly aroused both by English intervention in Scottish affairs and by the effect that this was likely to have on the attitudes of the people. The apparent English assumption that the Scots could not be trusted to deal with their own problems was humiliating. Were we too stupid, incompetent or dishonest? Over time this was a process that could undermine Scottish self-confidence. The acceptance for years of the two obvious distortions of the facts, which I have described, suggests that this is what in fact happened.

Inevitably the publication of the *Malachi Letters* created an immediate reaction. Petitions against the proposed law on banknotes flooded into Parliament from all parts of Scotland and the proposed legislation was soon withdrawn. Hugh MacDiarmid has said that Scott's argument 'leads naturally on to the separatist position', meaning Scottish independence[33]. But it was a very slow process. Increasingly in the 19th century attention concentrated on the Empire and not on Scotland itself. The *Malachi Letters* themselves, although the most pungent and outspoken of all Scott's works, became the least well known. It was a virtual censorship.

The Consequences of the Empire

In the course of the 19th century the Empire greatly stimulated the Scottish economy as a source of raw materials and a market for exports. Many Scots made a fortune in trade. Others had brilliant careers in the administration, development and defence of the Empire, which became unmistakably a British, and not only an English, enterprise. All of this was a consequence of the Union which, for that reason, became much more acceptable to Scottish opinion, almost beyond criticism.

At the same time, concentration on the Empire had disadvantages. People flooded from the countryside to the towns in search of employment. Scotland had no authority to deal with the social problems which followed from over-crowding, poor housing, unemployment and poverty. Over two million Scots emigrated between 1815 and 1939. We have still found no solution to the consequences of all of this.

The Empire dissolved rapidly after World War II as the former colonies became independent. Paradoxically, Wales and Scotland, which in a sense are the oldest colonies, are still for most purposes under the control of the Westminster Parliament in which their MPs are a small minority. If the Empire benefited Scotland in the days of the Empire, is there any case for it when the Empire no longer exists?

Resurgence

Towards the end of the 19th century there was a resurgence in both cultural and political self-confidence. There is always a close relationship between them. In the 1880s the Scottish Home Rule Association was formed and the conference of the Scottish Liberal Party adopted for the first time the policy of Home Rule for Scotland; the office of Secretary of State for Scotland was restored; the Scottish National Portrait Gallery, the Scottish Text Society and the Scottish History Society were founded. R. L. Stevenson wrote *Kidnapped* and *The Master of Ballantrae*; William McTaggart was painting some of his finest pictures; Greig and Duncan collected 3,500 folk songs in Aberdeenshire alone. By 1895, Patrick Geddes was able to write in his periodical *Evergreen* of a Scots Renaissance, long before the term was applied to the movement associated with Hugh MacDiarmid. Geddes himself was a leader in this revival, devoted to the cause of escaping from 'the intellectual thraldom of London' and restoring the old sympathies between Scotland and continental Europe[34]. In 1889 the first of a series of Home Rule for Scotland Bills were presented to the House of Commons, They made steady progress until they were interrupted by the First World War.

This war inflicted great damage on Scotland which suffered a disproportionate rate of casualties. Some people had doubts about the possibility of a Scottish recovery. There is, for instance, a well-known passage at the end of Lewis Grassic Gibbon's novel, *Sunset Song*, where he speaks of four of his characters, farm workers from the Mearns, who were killed in France:

> With them we may say there died a thing older than themselves, these were the Last of the Peasants, the last of the Old Scots folk. A new generation comes up that will know them not, except as a memory in a song.
>
> ... It was the old Scotland that perished then, and we may believe that never again will the old speech and the old songs,

the old curses and the old benedictions, rise but with alien effort to our lips[35].

In 1935 Edwin Muir made a tour through Scotland which he described in his book, *Scottish Journey*. He drew the conclusion from the experience that Scotland 'is now falling to pieces, for there is no visible and effective power to hold it together'[36]. Several other writers reached a similar conclusion.

But there were already other forces at work determined to prevent such a disaster. The Scottish National Party, devoted to the recovery of Scottish independence was founded in 1931. At about the same time many other organisations were established to encourage aspects of Scottish culture. They included the Scottish National Trust in 1932 to safeguard important Scottish buildings and countryside, and the Saltire Society in 1936, 'to encourage everything that might improve the quality of life in Scotland and restore the country to its proper place as a creative force in European civilisation'[37]. Other organisations were devoted to the Gaelic and Scots languages, literature and traditional music. At the same time, Hugh MacDiarmid stimulated both a literary and a political revival. The campaign to recover the Scottish Parliament, which began in the previous century, eventually succeeded with a decisive referendum in 1997. This was for a Parliament with strictly limited powers. The SNP campaigned for it because they thought it a step in the right direction, and Labour for the opposite reason that they hoped that it would discourage anything more ambitious.

The long period of subservience to the capital of another country with very different traditions and ideas from our own has inevitably had demoralising and debilitating consequences. Eric Linklater said in his book, *The Lion and The Unicorn:*

People degenerate when they lose control of their own affairs, and, as a corollary, resumption of control may induce regeneration. To any nation the essential vitamin is responsibility.

By reason of its association with England, Scotland

became insular. Its political frontier was broken down and its mind was walled up. Geographical or political enlargement, beyond certain limits, is nearly always accompanied by intellectual shrinkage[38].

I have already mentioned the adverse effects on our self-confidence of broadcasting controlled by London and of a curriculum in many schools which largely ignores our own history and literature and does its best to eradicate the Scots language. Broadcasting is probably the more damaging. It is a life-long influence after all and is probably the major one for most people. There are some good programmes but the vast majority ignore Scotland and take no account of our experiences and ideas. For this reason, the distinguished historian, Geoffrey Barrow, said that our failure to establish a Scottish organisation for public sector broadcasting was the greatest cultural disaster which Scotland suffered in the 20th century[39]. A senior official of the BBC said that it is the glue which held the Union together. It was presumably for this reason that when Labour drew up the Act to establish the devolved Scottish Parliament they made it responsible for cultural policy, but kept control of broadcasting, the most potent means of cultural expression, firmly in the hands of Westminster.

We can see the consequences of these influences in a report published in the Spring of 2008. This was the work of the Glasgow Centre for Population Health and NHS Health Scotland[40]. They found that life expectancy was shorter in the West of Scotland than in the most deprived areas of Eastern Europe and was improving more slowly than anywhere else. This has been attributed to low self-esteem, pessimism and lack of ambition, attitudes which are particularly acute in the West probably because of the decline in traditional industries. There was a time when Glasgow built a large proportion of the world's steam ships and railway locomotives and steel and coal mining were flourishing industries in the West of Scotland. Ship building is a shadow of its former self and the rest have virtually disappeared. The drift of ownership and control to the south has added to the decline. Such a major and long neglected problem demands the attention of a Scottish Government with the powers of independence.

We also need to improve the quality of our intellectual response to our problems. Broadcasting can help, but in both radio and television it has sharply deteriorated in recent years. News programmes often concentrate, not on important events, especially if they are in other countries, but on crime, the pointless activities of so-called celebrities and sport. There are very few programmes which show intelligence and an attempt to deal seriously with serious subjects. Perhaps this is a reflection of the current taste of the London audience. I am optimistic enough to think that we shall do much better in Scotland when we have our own public service broadcasting organisation. I hope that it would reflect our traditional enthusiasm for education, the democratic intellect, philosophical thought, scientific discovery and international relations. It is significant that the best BBC television programme on developments in Europe is the one in Gaelic.

Independence will not only make Scotland more prosperous and self-confident, but it will also help us to make a contribution, as in the past, to the development of other countries, in political and social ideas and in literature and the arts. Scotland will be a useful member of the European Union and the United Nations. Independence will also greatly improve our relations with England by removing the grievances caused by the Union and increased by Devolution. It is, for example, unacceptable that Members of the Westminster Parliament for Scottish constituencies can vote on matters affecting only England. Independent Scotland will be able to speak for its own interests in the Councils of Europe. On issues where we agree, which will be most of them, we shall have a stronger influence as two members than we have at present as one. As two independent neighbours, Scotland and England will have a close and friendly relationship when we are free from the irritations and complications of a Union which no longer has a useful purpose for either of us.

The experience of an SNP Government devoted to the radical improvement of conditions in Scotland has transformed the political situation. The advantages of independence are so great and so obvious that it cannot be long before we demand it in a referendum. At my age, I only hope that I live long enough to see it.

The New Situation

Events at Westminster in 2010 have made it even more urgent that Scotland should be liberated from its control. For ages the self-confidence of the Westminster Parliament has been so assured that it has persuaded the world at large that it is the ideal model of democracy in practice. That has always been far from the truth. There are many absurdities at Westminster such as the expensive play-acting of the State Openings, but the major objection is precisely its undemocratic structure. It has an electoral system which gives power not to the party with the largest number of votes but of seats won. As Tom Nairn points out, the Labour Government elected in 2005 had only 21.5 per cent of the votes. The Prime Minister so elected is a virtual dictator as long as he has control of his own party. There is a second chamber in the Lords, but it is not elected and the Prime Minister can appoint members to it.

Even after Devolution this undemocratic Parliament, in which the Scottish members are outnumbered ten to one, can impose policies on Scotland to which the majority of the Scottish people are opposed. They include such objectionable measures as nuclear submarines on the Clyde and the war in Iraq.

The Scottish Parliament – restored in 1997, but with very limited powers – has avoided many of the defects of Westminster. Its electoral system is not perfect but it is more democratic than at Westminster. Committees at Holyrood are more effective and the Parliament is much more open to public participation through the petitions procedure and the Cross Party Groups. A Conservative with experience of both Parliaments, 23 years as an MP and 8 as an MSP, James Douglas-Hamilton devotes several pages of his recent autobiography to praising the ways in which Holyrood is superior.

The long established self-confidence of Westminster was finally shattered in 2009 by the massive scandal over the abuse of the system of allowances by many MPs. It is clearly now intolerable that such an organisation should continue to be the overriding authority for the government of Scotland.

Two very relevant comments have appeared recently in the press. The *Sunday Herald* of 28 February 2010 had an article by Michael Fergus, the founding partner of an economic consultancy in Scandinavia. It ended with the following paragraph:

> My experience of Norway is that independence would give a country like Scotland a completely different voice and influence in the world. Instead of relying on others to speak for us, Scotland would be able to actively shape the world through targeted diplomatic, cultural and commercial campaigns led by Scots.

Scotland has had a close relationship with Norway for many centuries. We are neighbours across the North Sea and in the past travel across water was easier than by land. Many Scots have played an important part in Norwegian life. Their greatest composer, Edvard Grieg, was of Scottish descent. Petter Dass, the son of Peter Dundas of Dundee, is celebrated in Norway as 'the father of Norwegian vernacular poetry'. Like Scotland, Norway lost its independence for several centuries. This was first to Denmark in 1397 and that lasted until 1814, a period which the Norwegians call 'the 400 years night'. Then, as part of the settlement after the Napoleonic War, sovereignty passed to the King of Sweden. The Norwegian Parliament campaigned for independence and that was achieved in 1905.

Norway has the disadvantages of being further north than Scotland and being more mountainous, but since it regained independence it has become one of the most prosperous countries in the world. This is mainly due to the discovery of oil in Norwegian waters. Part of the income from this has been used for the improvement of communications, especially the construction of many bridges to the islands, and part has built up a massive fund to sustain future prosperity. Scotland also discovered oil in her part of the North Sea at about the same time, but the proceeds have disappeared into the coffers of Westminster. Still, an unknown amount of this oil remains in our waters, and obviously this means that the sooner we achieve independence the better.

The other press comment was in Ian Bell's essay in *The Herald* of 27 February 2010:

> It would be a historic mistake for Scotland to fail to regain its independence in the modern world. The alternative is slow and inexorable decline. And we have done that.

We certainly have. Before the First World War Scotland was prosperous with thriving industry. We produced a large part of the world demand for steamships and railway locomotives. We had flourishing coal mines and steel mills under Scottish ownership and management. Now very little remains. Emphasis and activity has moved south. This is the consequence, and it is perhaps even democratically proper, of a British Parliament in which the Scottish members are outnumbered ten to one. Ian Bell is right. Without independence decline is inevitable.

The Westminster election of 6 May 2010 saw the installation of David Cameron as the Prime Minister of a Conservative-Liberal Democrat Coalition. He has kept his promise to visit our First Minister and give us an assurance that he would treat Scotland with respect. This is certainly an improvement on the open hostility of Labour. But at the same time Cameron also said that he would 'never give ground on his commitment to keep the United Kingdom together'. As Harry Reid says, it would make political sense for him to get rid of Scotland and its anti-Tory voters. Perhaps the Tories have an emotional need to cling to Scotland, Wales and Northern Ireland as the last remaining parts of a once great Empire. On the other hand, Labour has a strong compulsion to keep Scotland in the Union as an important source, so far at least, of Labour votes.

As the price of coalition, the LibDems have surrendered, or post-poned, many of their cherished policies on constitutional reform and the abolition of Trident. On many of these issues there is close agreement with the policies of the SNP, except the important difference that they want federation, not Scottish independence. In fact, England is so much larger than the other parts of the UK, and shows no disposition to divide itself into smaller units, that federation would make no sense. It would leave England in control of foreign affairs and defence and we should therefore continue to be liable to such misfortunes as Trident submarines and involvement in the Iraq war. Scotland is larger and more developed than many of the other long submerged nations in Europe which have now recovered their independence and become full members of the EU and other international organisations. Scotland has the need and the right to follow their example.

As Alyn Smith MEP, an SNP member of the European Parliament, said recently:

> As the EU becomes, quietly, more and more relevant to our lives, the more people the length and breath of Europe are realising that this makes independence a necessity. To play a full part in the EU we must have the freedom to be ourselves, and right now we are represented by London and too often the London Minister barely thinks about us at all. It is laughable that Malta with fewer people than Edinburgh, and Estonia, Latvia and Lithuanian with fewer than Glasgow are all at the top table while we sit outside. The clearest case for independence is in Brussels.

Then there is the deplorable conduct of the Labour opposition in the Scottish Parliament since the SNP became the Government in the election of 2007. Under the lamentable leadership of Iain Gray they have automatically opposed most proposals of the SNP, without regard to its desirability or necessity. Joyce McMillan wrote in *The Scotsman* of 12 November 2010:

This time around the worst culprits were the dismal Labour group in the Scottish Parliament, so doggedly opposed to every suggestion from the SNP government that they would rather take the side of corporate power than act to protect the health and welfare of the people. Their forefathers from the old temperance movement, which helped to found the Labour Party, would blench in shame at their pathetic complicity with the big boys of the alcohol industry.

February 2011 was a devastating month for the Labour Party in Scotland. On Tuesday 16 *The Times* published the results of an opinion poll under the heading '*Salmond surges into a Holyrood lead*'. There had been very few polls on Scottish politics, but as recently as November 2010 polls had shown Labour with a ten-point lead over the SNP. In the new poll the SNP is ahead of Labour, if only slightly, giving the SNP 51 seats in the Scottish Parliament and 48 to Labour. On the following day *The Scotsman* reported that their research had shown that although Salmond was well known and respected, Iain Gray, the Labour leader, was hardly known at all. On the same day, under the headline 'Labour is stunned' it reported that Wendy Alexander, the previous Labour leader, had decided to abandon politics to spend more time with her children. All of this only three months before the Scottish Election in May.

Fortunately, this Election will give the Scottish people an opportunity to confirm their approval of Alex Salmond and his strong team.

Notes

1   E. F. Schumacher, *Small is Beautiful,* (London, 1974) Reprint of 1977, pp.52–3

2   *Key Facts and Figures about Europe and the European Union,* (Luxembourg, 2007. Office for Official Publications of the European Union)

3   David Hume, *Selected Essays,* ed. Stephen Copley and Andrew Edgar, (Oxford, 1993) p.311

4   Adam Ferguson, *An Essay on the History of Civil Society,* 1767, ed. Duncan Forbes. (Edinburgh, 1966) p.59

5   E. F. Schumacher, *Small is Beautiful,* (London, 1974) Reprint of 1977, p14

6   Johan P. Olsen in *The Future of the Nation State* ed. Sverker Gustavsson and Leif Lewin, (London 1996) pp.274–5

7   Poul Schlüter, in *Analysis* on BBC Radio 4, 19 September 1991

8   Garret Fitzgerald in *Scotland on Sunday,* 30 April 1989

9   Mary Robinson in *The Scotsman,* 29 June 1992

10 Hume Brown, *The Union of 1707.* (Glasgow, 1907) p.4

11 Iain Banks in *Edinburgh Evening News,* 15 March 2008

12 *The Herald,* 29 December 2005 and 30 January 2006

13 *The Herald,* 21 January 2007

14 *The Scotsman,* 30 March 2008

15 *The Scotsman,* 31 March 2008

16 Emile Noel in *Scotland on Sunday,* 5 March 1989 and *The Scotsman,* 12 June 1989

17 Alexander Broadie, *The Tradition of Scotish Philosophy* (Edinburgh, 1990) p.3

18 T. B. Macaulay, *History of England* (London, 1858) Vol.IV. pp.782–3

19 Harold Orel, *The Scottish World: History and Culture of Scotland* (London, 1981) p.12

20 Arthur Herman, op.cit. (London, 1981) p.12

21 J. A. Froude quoted by Prof. Gordon Donaldson in his Inaugural Lecture in the University of Edinburgh, 1964

22 Michael Hechter, op.cit. (London, 1973) pp.64, 73, 80

23 J. Derrick McClure in *Why Scots Matters* (4th edition, Edinburgh, 2008)

24 Linda Colley in *Britons: Forging the Nation, 1707–1837* (Yale, 1992) p.130

25 Adam Smith, *Correspondence,* ed. E. C. Mosner and I. C. Ross. (Glasgow, 1994) p.68

26 Henry Cockburn, *Journal. 1831–54.* (Edition of 1874, Edinburgh) Vol.I, p.37

27 Harold Macmillan in *Talking About Scott*, ed. Ian Campbell and Peter Garside, (Edinburgh, 1994) p.49

28 J. G. Lockhart, *Memoirs of Sir Walter Scott*, (Edition of 1900, London) Vol.I, p.460

29 Sir Walter Scott, *Tales of a Grandfather*, (Edition of 1889, Edinburgh) p.770

30 Angus Calder, *Revolving Culture*, (London and New York, 1994) p.69

31 Sir Walter Scott, *Letters*, ed. by H. J. C. Grierson., (London, 1935) Vol.IX, p.437

32 Sir Walter Scott, *The Letters of Malachi Malagrowther*, ed. by P. H. Scott, (Edinburgh, 1981) pp.9–10, 136–137, 143, 72

33 Hugh MacDiarmid, *Lucky Poet*. (London, 1943) p.203

34 Patrick Geddes quoted in Philip Mairet, *Pioneer of Sociology: The Life and Letters of Patrick Geddes*, (London, 1957) p.68

35 Lewis Grassic Gibbon, *Sunset Song*, (in the Trilogy Edition, *A Scots* Quair, London, 1971) p.193

36 Edwin Muir, *Scottish Journey*, (Edition of 1979, Edinburgh) p.25

37 Saltire Society Syllabus 2007–8

38 Eric Linklater, *The Lion and the Unicorn*, (London, 1935) pp.26, 130

39 Geoffrey Barrow in a lecture to the Saltire Society

40 *Sunday Herald*, 6 April 2008 and BBC Newsnight Scotland, 7 April 2008

CHAPTER 2

Make a Noble Dream Come True

HARRY REID

A Romp Through 304 Years

THE UNION BETWEEN England and Scotland in 1707 created the British state, and the British state is clearly in terminal decay. It is not working; it is not serving its people adequately. Many of its citizens are unaware of any meaningful concept of British nationhood. Far less do they believe in any such concept. Meanwhile the leaders of the UK are essentially engaged in the management of decline and they are not even very good at that. The break-up of the British state would give Scotland a splendid chance to regroup, to renew, to build and to roll out an improving and forward-looking society. And that applies to England too.

Yet many people wish to cling onto the British state. This suggests a failure of vision, certainly a failure of imagination. It also speaks of a mixture of complacency, conservatism, fear of change and timidity, which in turn perhaps reflects the rather cowed condition of a state mired in incompetence and full of doubt and even shame.

In its early days, in the 18th century, the British state was characterised by venality, duplicity and incompetence on a spectacular scale. The terms of the Union itself were broken early on: for example, Scottish landowners were given the right to appoint parish ministers, a breach of the Union settlement which to many Scots was contentious, offensive and provocative. How could this happen in direct contravention of the Union agreement? The answer is that the English had in effect taken over Scotland.

The man who to all intents dominated the British state in its early years was the first British prime minister. An Englishman called Sir Robert Walpole, he was an egregious rogue, one of the most corrupt political leaders in European history. Most of his successors were, if not as corrupt, weak and incompetent.

Among the 'achievements' of the British state in its first century was the repression of the Scottish Highlands after the failed Jacobite rebellion of 1745–6. The majority of Scots did not support the Jacobites, but the post-Culloden breaking up of Scottish Highland society was unnecessarily vicious and vindictive. Another 'achievement' was the loss of the American colonies. The British state wanted to retain these colonies and their loss was a debacle characterised by serial political bungling and compounded by crass military incompetence.

In the latter part of the century the early stirrings of industrialisation anticipated the huge social and economic revolution which made Britain the manufacturing centre of the entire world. This was partly the consequence of superb natural resources in Scotland and England, especially the rich coalfields, and the emergence of a breed of brilliant engineers, inventors and entrepreneurs, some of them men of little education who excelled at improvisation. One such was the canal builder of genius James Brindley who revolutionised the internal transport system through much of England. Many of these remarkable figures were Scots.

The Union had undoubtedly provided a significant tariff-free internal market, while the nascent Empire was to provide further economic opportunity abroad. But at the same time the social consequences of all this, not least mass migration to ill planned new cities, were often catastrophic. The industrial revolution, as it came to be called, was blemished by the systematic exploitation of very cheap labour. The British state was for at least three generations utterly unable to deal with the social effects of the creation of the first large-scale modern proletariat.

As well as inventors, industrialists and engineers of genius, Britain was producing outstanding thinkers, writers and reformers. Scotland provided more than her fair share of this special breed. A topical exemplar was Adam Smith, the Scottish philosopher and economist who was perhaps the supreme theorist of markets and capitalism.

Also in the ranks of these thinkers and writers were many radical and far-sighted subversives. Too often, if understandably, the British state regarded them as enemies. An example was Tom Paine, who played a significant role in both the American and French revolutions and to this day remains a hero in the US and France. (In Britain he is virtually forgotten – the British have to a large extent lost their sense of history).

Paine was tried in Britain, though he was exiled, for sedition. The British state was determined to crush him. The chief prosecutor, a future British prime minister, described Paine as wicked and malicious. The jury, picked by the Government, did not even bother to hear the judge's summing up, they were so eager to pronounce Paine guilty. He was sentenced to death. Such bitterly inglorious episodes were all too common.

Eventually, in the Victorian era, there was at last a realistic state response to the colossal social evils created by massive and rapid industrialisation. It was a miracle that there had not been a full scale revolution.

Meanwhile the British Empire was stretching across the globe. I do not want to get into the debate about whether the British were good or bad imperialists. The audit on the imperial legacy must be mixed. But two points are crucial. It was not an unmitigated success, and the legacy is often depressing.

For example if we look at two rogue states which are causing much anguish in the world today because of their reckless disregard for civilised behaviour to their own citizens – Zimbabwe and Burma – we can see the grievous long-term consequences of failed British imperialism. Secondly, the spectacular speed at which the Empire was lost in the second part of the 20th century was a major contributor to a loss of self-confidence in Britishness, though this was perhaps less of a factor in Scotland.

The early years of the 20th century were marked by the eminently avoidable disaster of the First World War, which was a catastrophe for Britain. Many of its best young men did not return from four years of pointless carnage. Those who did return from the 'war to end all wars' did not come back to a land fit for heroes. They returned to a state which was torn apart by industrial strife, including the first general strike, ever rising unemployment and increasing social faction and division.

Indeed I would argue that the British state only really came good in the middle of the 20th century, when there were two significant, and in different ways glorious, developments. Galvanised by a one-off war leader of unsurpassed genius, Winston Churchill, the British people defied the unique and heinous menace of Nazism, and for a time stood alone against that evil. When the Nazi war machine had at last been defeated (not least by the Americans and the Russians), the British state was exhausted.

Then came the second development, in its different way almost as remarkable. Despite its impoverished post-war condition, the British people found the courage to embark on a huge social experiment, the creation of a colossal 'welfare state'. The guiding genius was the Liberal politician William Beveridge, who wanted to eliminate the giant evils he identified in British society: Want, Disease, Ignorance, Squalor and Idleness. It was a vastly expensive and nobly motivated experiment, all the more impressive for being launched by a state that was virtually bankrupt after a heroic war effort.

The experiment has been at best a mixed success. On many tests, not least the elimination of Beveridge's five evils, it has been a failure. Nonetheless when it was launched by the socialist government of Clem Attlee, it was a brave and progressive experiment. Professor Tom Devine has argued that in Scotland the introduction of interventionist social policies guaranteeing decent standards of living helped to mitigate the effects of loss of Empire. The welfare state became the defining essence of the British state.

Thus the 1940s were a remarkable decade, and for me these years marked the last high point of Britishness. The magnificent generation who were in their prime then have been sadly passing away. This is of great significance when we observe the contemporary crisis of the British state. The fact that many of the generation who fought the war and created our welfare state are now dead while those of them who are still alive are seniors and will not be with us for much longer has profound significance.

These are the people for whom the Union had a particular resonance; the 'think of what we've all been through together' generation. For many of them, the British state is understandably something to be proud of. And again for them, two components of the British state, the monarchy and the armed forces, have special emotional resonance.

But in the 1950s a rapid decline set in. Britain became much less important in the world, even in Europe. The British state was not just losing its Empire; its great wartime ally, the US, was increasingly indifferent; and the rising states of the new Europe were aloof and disdainful.

The British state did maintain its supposedly independent nuclear deterrent which guaranteed it a place at the world's top table, via permanent membership of the UN Security Council, but that merely masked (very expensively) the reality of pervasive decline. Further, the main base for the 'deterrent' was in Scotland, which made Scotland a prime target during the Cold War.

There was in the 1950s and even more obviously in the 1960s, a failure of national confidence. British nationhood became something to be scorned and mocked rather than admired. The slick Tory showman Harold Macmillan preached a cynical consumerist paean to brittle short term affluence ('You've never had it so good' was his most famous, or rather infamous, slogan) in order to disguise the loss of power, esteem and national confidence. Socially the British became less cohesive; satire and permissiveness undermined what older citizens regarded, vaguely, as core British values.

The first great shock to British self-esteem had come with the Suez debacle of 1956; many more were to follow. Six of the leading countries on the continent formed the European Common Market; Britain first stayed aloof, and then desperately tried to join, only to be snubbed by the French. This was a terrible blow to British *amour propre*, if that is the appropriate phrase.

In the 1970s several eminent and distinguished observers thought Britain was becoming ungovernable. In 1976 the Labour government so mismanaged the British state's finances that it had to borrow, in humiliating desperation, huge amounts of money from the International Monetary Fund and from West Germany. This was at the very time when North Sea oil revenues were beginning to cascade into the British state's coffers. The paradox was not lost on many perceptive Scots. The slogan 'It's Scotland's oil' had a potent and legitimate resonance.

At this time a group of Scottish Nationalist MPs had been elected to the Westminster Parliament. One of them, the redoubtable Winnie Ewing, later described most of the Unionist MPs who were representing Scottish seats as boorish mediocrities. She was especially contemptuous of the Labour MPs. 'I'd look at the ranks of these people in the debating chamber. I thought: My God, these people are representing my country, they are representing Scotland. In these days many Labour activists in Scotland, and even more Labour voters, were decent hardworking people. Yet the people they elected were often third-raters'.

I think her strictures are justified, though I'm sure that at least some of the Scottish Labour MPs were decent, industrious politicians. One such was Frank McElhone, who represented the Gorbals area in Glasgow. I got to know him well when I was working as an education journalist; Frank was for a time Scottish education minister in the Callaghan government. Publicly, Frank always averred that Labour would deliver for the people of Scotland; privately he was less certain.

He told me more than once that he feared for the future of the city he loved, Glasgow. He believed that there was what he called a diaspora of the 'virile working class' (Frank was never politically correct) to the various Scottish new towns. He feared that many of the families left in Glasgow would break up, and many of its citizens – hundreds of thousands of them – would become wholly dependent on the state.

Yet he conceded that the state could never sustain all these people's needs. He set up a kind of one-off, supercharged citizens' support bureau, known as Frank's Bank, in the Gorbals, partly to cut through state bureaucracy. He believed passionately in the welfare state; at the same time he admitted that for many of his constituents, it wasn't delivering.

Meanwhile in London one of the most able of the Nationalist MPs, the late Douglas Henderson, was asked to characterise how the two great Unionist parties, the Tories and Labour, reacted to a well organised group of Nats at Westminster. He replied in one word: 'Horror'.

The Labour Government of the late 1970s not only grievously mishandled Britain's finances; it also presided over a calamitous collapse in industrial relations. Public strife escalated, culminating in the 'winter of discontent' when, at one point, the dead were not buried.

This spiral of political and economic decline was partly reversed by the belated arrival of a strong leader, Margaret Thatcher; the most significant figure by far in the recent history of the British state. She had many impressive qualities, not least courage and conviction, compared to her predecessors Callaghan, Wilson, Heath, Douglas Home, Macmillan and Eden, who were all essentially third or fourth-rate leaders, but she was also a disastrously divisive force within the British state.

In Scotland she was detested. She was perceived as anti-Scottish, a view that was compounded when Scotland was selected as a kind of testing ground for her hated 'poll tax'. Whether she meant to or not, she did enormous damage to the already fragile cohesion of the British state. In Scotland, respect for and belief in the Union was now more strained than ever.

It was in 1979 that Margaret Thatcher became leader of a state that appeared near to breakdown. She applied much tough medicine to the confused and stricken patient but she was in no way a gentle or caring physician.

All this meant that the concept of 'Britishness' was becoming almost impossible to nurture. As noted above, one or two British institutions – notably the monarchy and our armed forces – still held an emotional resonance for many older British citizens in a way that seemed to endorse British values as being decent, strong and worthy of patriotic pride.

But other British institutions, including the Westminster Parliament itself, were regarded with growing contempt. When the precocious Scottish Labour politician Gordon Brown, who was later to become a beleaguered and inept leader of the British state, was desperately looking for something to serve as a benign and positive focus for Britishness, he seized on the National Health Service, the key component in the welfare state that had been created in the 1940s. It was significant that he did not refer to the British Parliament which had been created so many years earlier.

That most perceptive of contemporary journalists, Neal Ascherson, has closely observed these eddies and tides in the affairs of the British state. In his 2006 Orwell Lecture Ascherson reflected on how Gordon Brown, as we have just seen, seized on the National Health Service as 'a common achievement, a great moral reform' as he searched for a fitting object of British patriotism. Ascherson claimed that this was actually the most impressive thought Brown had ever put forward. But he went on to note that in a later interview with the right-wing *Daily Telegraph*, Brown praised the British patriotism of Churchill and Thatcher – but nobody in his own party.

He celebrated 'British virtue' as 'liberty married to social responsibility and a belief in what Churchill called fair play'. Ascherson, then wryly noted that this was 'attractive, but not solid enough to form the pedestal for a new patriotism'.

I personally believe that any meaningful notion of British patriotism is now virtually defunct. Yet the idea of Scottish patriotism, and indeed the idea of English patriotism, are both alive and well. They could and should be harnessed by benign and progressive politicians.

This romp through the 304 years of 'British' history is a story of both significant achievement and appalling defeat. It is a narrative marked by interludes of glory, but marred by persistent failure and growing decline. I have tried to be careful to give the English their due; they are in so many ways a magnificent people. They have produced more than their fair share of geniuses and authentic world figures. Shakespeare and Newton must surely be among the handful of utterly momentous world-changing, world-enhancing human beings.

Further, the authors of the many problems of the British state have been Scottish as well as English. Many Scottish politicians in both the Labour and Tory parties have over the years been culpable, in that they have directly contributed to the decline of the British state, whose main hallmark is now a corrosive and constant incompetence.

I have above cited as examples of British individual greatness the engineer Brindley, the writer and thinker Paine, the war leader Churchill; this is not to defer to the English, but rather to indicate that they have consistently produced men and women of genius who have contributed enormously to the British state, and beyond. Whatever this essay is about, it is not about any glib anti-Englishness, any disdain for English achievement.

But since the 1950s Britain has produced far fewer outstanding individuals and, as I have tried to indicate, the British state has become mired in decline. The decay noticeably set in at the time of the Suez fiasco and has been accelerating ever since. My contention is simple: the British state is spent.

On the other hand I do not wish to exaggerate; British citizens still live in a free and relatively stable society. But they are not as confident, happy, prosperous and ambitious as they should and could be. They are less well educated than they might be; their behaviour is increasingly self indulgent, anarchic and turbulent; and their future looks problematic. Too many of them are almost encouraged by the state to leech off that very state; Britain has a huge number of young people who are not in education, employment or training. Others, often those at the bottom of the heap, are given scant support or assistance by the state in their daily struggle.

Obviously constitutional change cannot of itself solve these issues, but it can act as an enabler. It can provide the platform for significant revival.

The British state, so adept at printing money – or 'quantative easing' to use the state's own preferred, pretentious and evasive euphemism – in the months before the 2010 general election, proved rather less efficient at printing ballot papers. Well, money no doubt comes before democracy.

Towards the end of Election Day, Thursday 6 May 2010, various polling stations across England ran out of ballot papers. Almost as bad, many other polling stations were seriously understaffed and voters who in some instances turned up more than an hour before polling was due to close were denied their democratic right as long queues had formed.

Some of these local debacles were observed by monitors from emerging countries, in Britain to see an allegedly mature democracy in action. Alas, the failing British state could not even manage the basic mechanics of an honourable election.

As for the actual result, it presented in the sharpest of relief what had for some time become ever more evident – that the United Kingdom was totally disunited. The divergence between the key component parts of Scotland and England was now even more marked than before. England, which had narrowly voted Tory in 2005 – only to be denied by cohorts of Labour votes elsewhere – swung more enthusiastically towards the Tories.

Even in industrial and post-industrial seats in the North of England, there were some very strong swings to the Tories. But in similar industrial and post-industrial seats over the Border, Scotland remained solidly and defiantly Labour.

Despite this, the new leader of the British state, David Cameron, was true to his word. He had promised that if he became prime minister, he would visit Scotland within a week. Indeed Holyrood, not Westminster, was the first legislature that Cameron visited as PM.

For his first few days in office, Prime Minister Cameron was all sweetness and light. Gaining power on a hastily cobbled deal with the LibDems, he evinced a kind of crazed, courageous opportunism, while his utterances were soft and consensual.

On the whole, he received a good press in England. There was much talk of the 'new politics'. Same old Union, however, but the gaping divergence that was splitting the Union apart was, for the time being, conveniently forgotten. Some English commentators were ecstatic. Matthew Parris, a writer I respect, commented that the electoral outcome 'bordered on the supernatural'. He said that there had been 'a palpable lifting of ghastliness.'

David Cameron is an astute politician of sunny disposition but his tone changed subtly when he came north of the Border. He could not resist pointing out, as he emphasised his right to govern Scotland, that he and his new coalition partners, the LibDems, had won a higher proportion of votes than the SNP had when it took power in Holyrood in 2007.

This was technically correct. But those who voted SNP in 2007 knew what they were voting for. Whereas millions upon millions of those who voted Tory and LibDem in 2010 had no idea that they were voting for a coalition government, though this was what they got. The outcome may have been 'bordering on the supernatural' for some venerable English pundits, but masses of ordinary voters felt they had been duped.

Cameron deployed his considerable charm during his whistle-stop visit to Scotland on Friday 14 May 2010 as the new leader of the British state, yet the visit did not bode at all well. He seemed remarkably unconcerned about the abject, pitiful failure of his party in Scotland, where the Scots had returned the grand total of one Tory MP out of a possible 59.

How could anyone trumpet the integrity of the Union when so very many English folk voted Tory, and so pitifully few Scots?

Indeed in the intermediate aftermath of this extraordinary election, it appeared that the electoral cohesion of the Union had vanished. Some observers detected in Scotland a tendency to vilify the Tory Party that bordered on the tribal, or even the sectarian. It was as if hating the Tories was a psychological test you had to pass before you could be regarded as a proper Scot.

This pointed to resentment, even bitterness, yet it could be forgiven given the nonsensical political construct which Scots were now being asked to keep afloat. The paradox was that, by voting Labour in vast numbers, Scots were indeed keeping this hulking old ship the Union, afloat, just about. They were exposing the sham that the Union was, by diverging so spectacularly from their English counterparts; yet at the same time they were propping up the Union, for Labour in Scotland remained the nationalists' most virulent enemy.

The outcome also pointed to a rarely discussed factor; the risible and abject failure of the English Left. For too long the Left in England have been relying on Scots, and to a lesser extent, Welsh politicians to sustain Left of centre politics in the Union. So a crucial mid-term question in UK politics is this: Can the English Left find some way of reinventing itself, and soon?

Otherwise the Union will without doubt break up, with England consigned to be a more or less permanent Tory oligarchy, while Scotland and Wales will move forward as states of the soft Left.

It was not just in the 2010 general election that the Tories in England found themselves a majority in their own country, only to be denied the full prize by the anti-Tory voting of other parts of the Union. The process has been going on, with a few interruptions, for a very long time.

I did not hear it myself, but I was told that soon after the results of the 2010 general election were complete the BBC carried a radio broadcast from Henley in which baying English voices were beginning to voice serious indignation at this democratic deficit. Obviously I have an aversion to baying English voices articulating anti-Scottish sentiments but even so, as a democrat, I have every sympathy with the millions upon millions of English voters who are starting to believe themselves to be seriously, and possibly permanently, disenfranchised.

Well, there is an obvious and sensible answer to this conundrum: Break up the Union. If the English had England to themselves, they could vote Tory to their hearts' content: Problem over.

But there is an immediate difficulty with that. Many of these Tory-tending English voters have a potent, if utterly irrational, regard for the Union. Their current leader and spokesman David Cameron typifies this. I called him astute. However this astuteness deserts him when it comes to the Union.

It makes political sense for him to get rid of Scotland and its cussedly anti-Tory voters, yet he cannot bring himself to try to do so because of some atavistic and inexplicable veneration for the Union. You could almost admire him for his loyal attachment to a chimera which prevents him and his party from holding absolute sway in England, but you have to wonder at his political sense, or lack of it.

It is extraordinary that within England meaningful challenges from the Left have persistently come NOT from within England but from elsewhere. I'm not just talking about the way the Scots and to a lesser extent the Welsh are able to impose on the colossal cadres of English Tory governments they do not want and certainly haven't voted for. I'm talking about political leadership.

Take the history of the Labour Party. Who are Labour's really towering, iconic figures? I'd say: Keir Hardie, Ramsay MacDonald (yes, I'm serious), Clem Attlee, Nye Bevan and Michael Foot. Just two Englishmen there, and Foot, Labour's only prophetic figure in recent times, the very embodiment of charismatic radicalism, was by any standards an adoptive Welshman. He was elected MP for Ebbw Vale, Nye Bevan's old constituency, in 1960 and for the next 50 years Wales was to be the spiritual as well as the political home of this passionate crusader of the Left.

Of course Foot was an ineffective leader. He had no answer to the sheer electoral popularity of Thatcherism in England (and remember that Thatcher, unlike Blair, won far more votes in her third general election victory than in her first)

Anyway, when Foot failed, the English Left turned to a real

Welshman, Neil Kinnock, a man who had been brought up in Nye Bevan's hometown, Tredegar, to fight Thatcher. Was no-one in England available?

So whether we like it or not, and most Scots don't, England fell in love with Thatcher. After she was discarded not by the English electorate, who almost certainly would have voted for her for a fourth time, but by a myopic mini-mob within her own party, the Tories lost their appetite for power, though John Major scrambled to an unlikely victory in 1992.

As the Tories became corrupt and rotten, a slick trio of political opportunists (Blair, Brown and Mandelson) worked out how to appeal specifically to England and the English. They knew that they could take control of the UK if they could fight the Tories at their own game. In other words, hijack the Labour Party, so popular in Scotland and Wales, so comparatively unpopular in England, and reinvent it as a sort of successor to Thatcherism, enough of a successor to con Middle England.

Thus the phoney construct of New Labour was invented, and it worked – for a time. Middle England fell for it. But of course this was not about giving the Left power in England: almost the opposite, in fact.

England was briefly persuaded by this cunning manoeuvre, and was prepared to give New Labour the benefit of the doubt in a couple of elections. But by the 2005 general election the English had seen through the trick, and reverted to type, voting Tory. New Labour could survive for another five years only because the Old Labour battalions in Scotland and Wales came, as so often, marching to the rescue. Then, in May 2010, the English decided they had had more than enough of New Labour.

It will be ironic indeed if the ultimate breakthrough is not a result of anything the Scots or Welsh achieve but rather because the English at long last decide they have had their fill of outsiders spoiling their Tory party.

But David Cameron continues to fight doggedly for the notion of

Britishness, despite the fact that he seems unable to define it himself, and despite the increasingly obvious perception that Britain is a failed state, a mere client of the increasingly disdainful Americans, and economically impotent in the face of the rising new world powers such as China, India and Brazil.

A corrosive sense of 'British' failure was growing. During the bad weather of December 2010 the British Airports Authority's inability to keep Heathrow Airport – Britain's flagship airport – open after a few inches of snow fell, provoked much visceral anger. Thousands of people were furious because they could not get away from Britain, which maybe said it all.

It was also noted that despite its name the British Airports Authority was in fact Spanish-owned; like so much that was British it had been sold off. The Heathrow debacle was regarded as national humiliation, but a British humiliation rather than an English humiliation.

When things go wrong, as they increasingly do in Britain, people's response seems to be less to regard England or Scotland as being incompetent or in decline; it is Britain that is blamed.

As if to combat this, David Cameron sought to flag up British identity. In a keynote speech – peculiarly delivered not in Britain but in Germany in February 2011 – he called for the renewal of a shared British national identity. He wanted young British males, in particular, to identify with the concept of Britain.

This exceedingly important speech was made in the context of a discussion of multiculturalism and Islamist extremism. This was doubly interesting. We all knew that Cameron was against Islamist extremism; many of us were unaware that he was so hostile to multiculturalism. Significantly, his attack seemed to be based on a revival of 'British' identity. Also significantly, he was suggesting that Britain had become too tolerant.

I, and no doubt millions of others, had been brought up to believe that Britain's supreme 'shared value' was that of tolerance. Now the leader of a coalition formed by two great British political parties, both with two centuries and more experience at the heart of the British state, was seeking to turn history on its head. Or was he?

In truth, it was a remarkable speech. With what sounded like a kind of cerebral longing, almost a yearning, for some cohesive and unifying values to define British identity, Cameron floundered around trying to home in on those elusive values. Yet this articulate, interesting and relatively young statesman seemed utterly unable to spell out in any detail exactly what these unifying British values were. Increasingly, there seemed to be at the core, the very heart of the British state, no heart at all – just a rather forlorn emptiness.

At the very time that Cameron was making his speech, it was leaked that the coalition government was considering the introduction of a new British national holiday in the autumn, to be designated as 'UK Day'. A Tory MP noted that it would be a 'very good idea to celebrate all things British'. All things British? What, exactly?

Meanwhile the Royal Family, the ultimate resort for those wishing to preserve the notion of Britishness at all costs, was being promoted as it had not been for generations. 2011 was to be the year of a much puffed royal wedding, with a British national holiday being held to celebrate the event – and the year of 2012 was to be devoted to the Queen's Diamond Jubilee, a year long Brit-fest in which appeals to British pride and patriotism would be unremitting. An over-hyped film about the Queen's father, which played fast and loose with historical reality, was widely acclaimed.

All this rather smacked of desperation, a defiant and cynical tilt against the anxieties and frustrations of a riven and weary people. To revive and re-energise the British people is simple; this will be achieved not by increasingly desperate stunts to foment Britishness, but rather by allowing the British state at last to dissolve.

Independence for Scotland is the case that is made forcefully and thoroughly in other essays in this book. They emphasise the positive. I'm convinced that the concomitant independence for England would also be liberating, an opportunity for renewal, for fresh thinking, for an inspiriting re-energising.

The British state has to be sent to the knacker's yard. But rotten and exhausted as it is, its proponents will not give up without a hard and logic-defying struggle.

CHAPTER 3

Scotland's Economic Options in the Global Crisis

STEPHEN MAXWELL

WHERE DOES THE economic case for Scotland's independence stand after the drama of the banking crisis?

'When the facts change, I change my mind. What do you do, sir?' asked Keynes. He must have known that such a straightforward principle does not apply in politics where changed facts are more likely to change arguments than conclusions.

Unionists argue that the collapse of Ireland's economy and the need of Scotland's two largest banks and private sector employers to be rescued by the UK Treasury have exposed the unreality of the SNP's case for Scottish independence. Supporters of independence argue that Scotland's exposure within the Union to the failures of UK economic and regulatory policies reinforce the case for independence. Service as usual.

The Unionists promote two lines of argument. The most common is that an independent Scotland could not have afforded to bail out its own banks and would have had to follow Ireland in accepting an EU and IMF bailout with the loss of sovereignty and all economic and social damage that entails. The second is that were Scotland to become independent in future, Scots taxpayers would have to carry by themselves the cost of the UK's £470bn financial salvage of the Scottish banks.

These claims provide Unionists with handy debating points but they unravel on analysis.

The first claim – that Scotland would have followed Ireland's path to financial ruin – rests on a long trail of assumptions. Its plausibility depends on a supposition that Scotland became independent on the very eve of the banking crisis burdened with the uncorrected legacy of its preceding decades of misgovernment by the UK. Even in its own terms this ignores important facts. First the rest of the UK would have been seriously exposed to the collapse of the Scottish banks by virtue of the sizeable proportion of their liabilities and staff located in the rest of the UK (rUK), principally England. In effect RBS and HBOS had ceased to be Scottish except by the location of their registered head-quarters. They were products of the Big Bang deregulation of the UK's financial sector in 1986 and were integrated with the rest of the UK's financial sector. In its own interest the rUK would have been impelled to share the costs of rescuing the Scottish banks.

Second, unlike Ireland, even a newly independent Scotland would have possessed its own insurance fund in the form of its North Sea oil reserves worth wholesale anything between £600bn and £1trillion. While the two Scottish banks' total liabilities were several times the value of Scotland's annual GDP they also had large stocks of sound assets, particularly RBS. The Treasury projected RBS capital losses at £60bn out of £282bn of assets placed by RBS in the Government's Asset Protection Scheme. By September 2009 actual losses amounted to £37bn. (National Audit Office, 2010). So even on this extreme hypothesis an independent Scotland would have been able to avoid Ireland's fate.

The assumption that Scotland became independent on the eve of the UK's banking crisis is just a piece of rhetorical self-serving. An alternative scenario could have located the moment of independence in say 1980 at the beginning of Scotland's role as a major oil producer. But Unionists would then have needed to deploy even more extravagant assumptions. Firstly, that through three decades of independence Scotland had followed the same path to banking crisis as the UK and Ireland. In this scenario Scotland would have squandered its oil wealth rather than used it to diversify Scotland's economy (as urged by the SNP at the time and endorsed by the then Chief Economic Adviser to the Scottish Office, Gavin McCrone, in his secret 1974 memorandum) in the process reducing the relative weight of financial services in the Scottish economy (Scottish Office, 1975). Secondly, that from 1997 Scotland would have followed the example of Gordon Brown's light touch regulation of the banks rather than the stricter regimes introduced by the Nordic countries following their financial crises in the late 1980s and early 1990s.

The second Unionist claim is that if Scotland were to become independent before the banks were free of the life support provided by the UK Government, Scottish taxpayers would have to shoulder the full cost of the UK's investment in and guarantees to the Scottish banks, estimated at £470bn. (Scottish Parliament, 2010). The liability is of course a possible cost: the real current cost is a fraction of the principal. This argument ignores the logic of the Union. Whatever the root causes of the banking crisis in the UK the public liability rests with the political authority with responsibility for regulating and supervising the banks. The responsible authorities were the UK Parliament and Government. Even the new leaders of the Labour Party have now acknowledged their Government's failure to regulate the banks adequately. Without any formal responsibility Scotland's responsibility is as part of the UK. Based on Scotland's shares of the UK's population or GDP, between 8–9 per cent, her share of the UK's liabilities might be £40bn. Such a sum would be an unwelcome addition to Scotland's legacy of national debt from the UK, currently around £80bn, but the cost would be manageable. In any case, short of a total collapse of the financial system, it remains hypothetical.

It is not surprising that financial crisis on the scale now facing many western economies has pushed the issue of risk to the forefront of the debate on Scotland's future. A more sophisticated Unionist interpretation of the financial collapse of Ireland and Iceland than the empty speculations peddled by the Unionist parties claims that the collapse demonstrates that under globalisation an independent Scottish economy would be exposed to an unacceptable level of financial risk.

But the relationship between the size of an economy and its exposure to risk of financial or broader economic collapse is not at all clear. True the larger a country's territory the more opportunities it might be expected to have to diversify its economy but the link is weak. In practice the exposure of any particular economy to risk depends on how well its people use their particular resources and opportunities. Well into the industrial age Finland and Norway were regarded as countries with limited economic prospects, but using what resources they had they have developed into highly successful post industrial states. They have had their share of crises and disasters along the way, but so have much larger states. It needs to be remembered that notwithstanding their current troubles, both Ireland and Iceland have enjoyed periods of great prosperity as independent states. Even in 2010 their capita GDP was higher than the UK's. (CIA World Factbook, 2011) Small economies may have a smaller margin for error in their economic and political decisions than larger states, but would anyone seriously argue that Ireland would have done better to remain under Westminster control or Iceland under Danish control, let alone that Norway would have done better under Swedish authority or Denmark as part of the German Confederation?

The chief executive of Ireland's central bank, Patrick Honohan, has seized on the collapse of the Irish banks as confirmation of his view that small countries should have foreign owners for their banks (Reuters, 24 November 2010). Given the way in which Ireland's bid to establish herself as a friendly offshore tax haven for foreign banks unravelled, most spectacularly with the collapse of Germany's Hypo Real Estates Irish arm Depfa in 2008, perhaps Dr Honohan should not be dumping all the blame on Irish controlled banks. His view condemns Ireland to be a perpetual dependant of global neo-liberalism. Like most small developed countries, the Nordic countries prefer to maintain nationally or jointly owned banks as the foundation of their banking system.

Dr Honohan must be gratified by the situation in Scotland where the combined effects of Mrs Thatcher's 1986 Big Bang liberalisation of financial services and two decades of light touch regulation has left the Airdrie Savings Bank, with eight local branches in its home region of Lanarkshire and a capital base of £130m, as the sole independent survivor of a once diverse and vigorous Scottish retail banking system. He will take further encouragement from the fact that no Scottish political party, not even the SNP, has shown any interest in rebuilding an independent Scottish banking system. The best that Scottish politicians appear to hope for is that new banks such as Tesco Bank and Virgin along with foreign based newcomers such as Santander will inject fresh competition into a Scottish market which since the restructuring of 2008 has been dominated by RBS and Lloyds TSB. On current policies if political Nationalism makes further progress Scotland could be the only European country in the modern age to approach independence without any nationally owned banks.

In Honohan's globalist vision this need not matter. In the absence of its own national banking system a small country can still have a Central Bank and, if a member of the Eurozone, a seat at the European Central Bank as well as at international forums for banking regulation. Currently Scotland lacks not only independent Scottish commercial banks but also, unlike most other developed economies, local savings banks, public pension backed regional banks specialising in infrastructure investment, mutual banks or charitable banks of significant size, or even, thanks to Treasury obstruction, a bond issuing agency for public infrastructure such as the originally conceived Scottish Futures Trust or a functioning State Development Bank. The result is a lack of competition in mainstream banking, a chronic scarcity of patient investment capital, an uncertain supply of venture capital and a dearth of development funding for small businesses, the third sector and communities, all contributing to a narrow and unstable Scottish financial base.

The apparent indifference of Scottish political opinion to the hollowing out of Scotland's financial system raises the question of how an independent Scotland would position itself in a globalised world in which neo-liberalism is the dominant ideology. While the crisis was a product of neo-liberalism the response of the West's political leaders has turned it into a crisis of social democracy. The money needed to bail out the banks is being found from cuts in the public services which are part of the foundations of social democracy. In the US a resurgent Republican Right is challenging Obama's progressivism. In the UK a new Centre Right Government is imposing cuts in public budgets worse than Mrs Thatcher's. Centre Right Governments rule in Germany and France. In Spain and Greece socialist Prime Ministers are bleeding the public sector to satisfy their international creditors and in last year's election even Sweden swung decisively to the right. Meanwhile the bankers who caused the crisis are escaping with their bonuses barely dented and their 'too big to fail' banks intact.

One Scottish commentator judges that social democracy is 'in tatters and retreat across the Western world' and concludes: 'Scotland cannot buck this development. We cannot be the land where time stood still'. (Hassan, Scotsman, 24 January 2011). Yet in planning its future as an independent state it would be perverse for Scotland to opt for the neo-liberal alternative which is the cause of the present crisis. The key principle of social democracy – that a democratic state has a responsibility to provide security and welfare for all its citizens – is more necessary than ever in a world buffeted by global market forces. The record of the Nordic countries in the last three decades shows that far from being a handicap in a globalised economy, social democracy offers the best chance for economic stability and social welfare. Even Sweden, the Nordic country which has shown the greatest tendency to challenge social democratic orthodoxy, has in its taxing and spending policies remained loyal to the Nordic model as against the liberal Anglo-American model represented by the USA, the UK and Ireland. (OECD, 2010).

This does not mean that social democracy, which devolved Scotland inherited from the United Kingdom, is an adequate foundation for an independent Scotland. It was too heavily imprinted with the centralising corporatism of Old Labour as well as being corrupted by New Labour's excessive deference to markets (Maxwell, 2007). While the first decade of devolution has improved the legacy in some important ways – easier public access to policy making, the introduction of STV for local elections, first steps towards direct community empowerment, setting boundaries to the role of markets in public services – it has failed to seize the potential for a second phase of devolution focused on the democratic empowerment of Scottish communities and civil society.

While more could have been achieved under devolution, the continuation of the Union undermines the political and social base for more radical reforms. For the second time in a generation Scotland is being forced by a UK Government, which Scots voters emphatically rejected at the polls, to inflict large cuts on the social democratic settlement favoured by the Scottish majority. Mrs Thatcher doubled Scottish unemployment and poverty. Whether David Cameron's even deeper cuts will wreak destruction on a comparable scale remains to be seen, but the economic cost to Scotland in the form of lagging investment in Scotland's economic potential, particularly in renewables, is already accumulating. As long as Scotland is exposed to the fickleness of middle England's political moods she will struggle to maintain the levels of capital and social investment necessary to repair the injuries inflicted by her history of industrialisation and deindustrialisation compounded by centuries of misgovernment from London. Even more damagingly, the economic and social effects of the cycles of right wing Government from England erode the confidence of Scots voters, fuelling those defensive reflexes which have regularly pushed them back to a Unionist Labour Party.

If the development of a bespoke version of social democracy balancing a strong national framework for economic development and social welfare with civil empowerment and the decentralisation of the management of public services is Scotland's best hope for the future, where is the space in a volatile global economy for such a project? The Union with England is evidently counterproductive. An enlarged European Union offers one option but, even before the banking crisis, the EU had begun to trim the disproportionate power small states enjoyed in the Union's decision making in response to enlargement. The Euro crisis is now directing the Union towards closer central control of the economies of Eurozone members. Like the Nordic countries, an independent Scotland could probably satisfy any strengthened economic criteria for Eurozone membership, at least after a transitional period. But it is doubtful whether membership of the Euro would best match Scotland's opportunities for national development. It is significant that of the four mainland Nordic countries only Finland is a member of the Eurozone. Assuming that the rUK remains outside the Euro, if the crisis forces the EU towards a two tier structure with membership of a more centralised Eurozone the dividing line between inner and outer circles, Scotland's best option would be in the outer circle allowing her to remain competitive with the rUK while providing maximum scope for developing her links with the Nordic countries. Whether Scotland then adopts sterling or, bolstered by rising world energy prices, opts for a separate Scottish currency would be a pragmatic judgement. Even if the rUK were to join the Eurozone, remaining outside the Euro, or even like Norway outside the European Union altogether, might offer Scotland more scope for the development of its social democratic project.

In *Ill Fares the Land*, the valedictory message of the late Tony Judt, the pre-eminent interpreter of Europe's post-war history, offers two key judgements: that after three decades of retreat in the face of globalisation the nation state is poised to reclaim a dominant role and that, in confronting the current crisis, nation states should look to social democracy as their route map, not because it represents an ideal future, even less an ideal past, but because it is better than anything else to hand. It is a message which should at once hearten and inspire the movement for Scottish independence.

References

National Audit Office (2010), *Report on the UK Treasury's Asset Protection Scheme,* HM Treasury, London.

Scottish Office (1975), *The Economics of Nationalism Re-Examined*, G. McCrone Scottish Economic Planning Department, Edinburgh.

The Times (7 May 2010), Interview with Alex Salmond.

Scottish Parliament (2010), *The Way Forward for Scotland's Banking, Building Society and Financial Services Sector,* Report by the Scottish Parliament Committee on the Economy, Energy and Tourism, Edinburgh.

Central Intelligence Agency 2010, *World Economic Factbook: Country Comparisons.*

Honohan P. Reuter's website, 24 November 2010.

Hassan G. *The Coming Scottish Revolution, The Scotsman,* 24 January 2011.

OECD (2010) *National Economic Statistics,* Paris.

Maxwell S. (2007) *The Voluntary Sector and Social Democracy in Devolved Scotland* in *Scottish Social Democracy: progressive ideas for public policy* ed. M. Keating PIE, Brussels 2007.

Judt Tony *Ill Fares the Land*, Allen Lane/Penguin Books, London 2010.

CHAPTER 4

Timed Out: Great Britain to Little England

TOM NAIRN

The G-B Election

SO THE GREAT-BRITISH General Election took place, on 6 May 2010. And on the seventh of May the voters woke up in Alice's Wonderland: 'Down, down, down. Would the fall *never* come to an end! I wonder how many miles I've fallen by this time?' she said aloud. 'I must be getting somewhere near the centre of the earth.' She worries about arriving among the 'Antipathies' on the other side, but the White Rabbit keeps reappearing and, in between nervous glances at his watch, reassures her things will soon be sorted out.

Today the White Rabbit is Nick Clegg, Leader of Britain's LibDems, summoned by 'the Duchess' (the Conservative Party's David Cameron) for grotesquely unlikely talks about common policy over staging the Mad Tea Party: dealing with Britain's gigantic deficit without turning the Pound Sterling into funny-money, being simultaneously for and against the European Union (and so on). Though uncomfortably like an accord between Albert Schweitzer and Genghis Khan, the deal does appear inevitable for the time being. The Conservative Party won most votes, and the LibDems have advanced sufficiently to claim a place at the power-table – or at least, for as long as Labourism continues to sink in the choppy wake of the departing Gordon Brown. Most recent reports indicate water-level rising near deck-level, and threatening the Bridge. However, what choice have the living but to seek an exit from zombiedom, however difficult?

In most countries, another election would be the answer. But this is Wonderland. A second contest might push everything still closer to the centre of the earth. Isn't the descendant of democracy succumbing to advanced Alzheimer's, and capable of results even worse than May the 6th? Hence, the urgent task ('national interest', etc.) boils down to getting rid of a millenary tradition in a few days: time to at least consider disposing of the Mother of Parliaments and 'first-past-the-post'. Reared to worship such timeless icons, today's Royal Subjects find themselves placed under brisk orders to bin the lot, and re-equip themselves for boring modernity. Two-partyism has joined the Dodo and the 'caucus race' in Dodgson's famous portrait of Englishness. As Iain Macwhirter concludes his 'State of the Nation' survey in Scotland's *Sunday Herald*: 'This election was a kind of punishment for the UK political leadership, for the expenses scandal and the banking crisis. The people wanted a change – well, now they have it. The political system is broken, but we don't yet know if anyone has the tools to fix it.' (9 May). That's the job of the incoming coalition government, and we're still finding out day by day just what the tools are, and how likely or unlikely will be the restoration of the historic United Kingdom.

The Missing Link

So far one thing has to be taken for granted: the absence of an *English* polity capable of asserting itself democratically, on behalf of its 85 per cent UK majority. No non-democratic or dictatorial alternative is yet presenting itself. Yet it should be more clearly recognised that what's happening *is* an odd sort of dictatorial solution: a power-system imposed by absence. Scottish, Welsh, Northern Irish and other peripheral opinion (e.g. the Isle of Man) are bound to react, but with no real option except one or other version of actual nationalism. In that sense, the latter turns out to be founded less on swelling separatist tides than on the hopeless breakdown of the centre, Westminster Britishness. Straightforward political reform, like proportional representation and federalism, has been put off too long.

And today no time is left. That is, no time for anything but panic and hasty makeshifts, manifested in the notion of a gambling-table deal between Deep-South Toryism and 'civic' Liberal Democracy, to keep catastrophe at bay. This *is* break-up, nor are we out of it. New Labour, 1997–2010, *was* the last chance saloon, and towards the end of it six-gun Brown couldn't even draw his shooter. Today we find him retired, but still leaning on the old bar without so much as a decent wise-crack to amuse the remaining soaks and newshounds. Out on Main Street, the contest is on for a British equivalent to Kevin Rudd.

Couldn't Labourism vote in another less Party-bound leader, and set up a different bar-room deal with the LibDems and the Scottish and Welsh Nationalists on all-round constitutional change – in effect, move towards some kind of confederal replacement for the United Kingdom? Possibly – but how many years could it take? The Britannic *ancien regime* is founded on the unthinkability of stuff like that. So it will have to emerge in fits and starts like those we're going through – over the wreckage of Gordon Brown's Britishness and David Cameron's smart new ways to keep the old Union going. Open Democracy and like-minded organs have been arguing in that general direction for decades already, preaching to the largely unconverted. Now suddenly everybody has experienced a five-minute conversion – forced on them by the simple failure and incapacity of the traditional regime. The question has turned from whether or not to be 'radical', into just which version of radicalism will best fit the new times. Against the grain of Britishness and most of the secular odds it imposed, a stalled evolutionism has ended by setting the stage for political revolution.

Conscious of approaching doom, Cameron's first move as Premier was to Scotland, where he commiserated with that country's Conservatives on their single constituency victory, and held awkward talks with the LibDems and Nationalists. Everyone is aware that the ruling Scottish Nationalists want a referendum on independence, and an end to the United Kingdom. Cameron has repeatedly stated that he doesn't want to go down in history as the last Prime Minister of Great Britain. But he also insists on a regime of 'respect' for the devolved governments. To mean anything, 'respect' entails equality, or the pretence thereof. But there can of course be no such equality between Britain and its 'component' parts. Unequalness is written into any union between an eighty-five per cent majority and assorted minorities with varying ethnic, linguistic and societal natures and ambitions. Standard-issue international relations are founded upon *formal* respect among such unequal entities – which of course entails the common ground of independence, recognition and statehood.

In the British case, such mutuality is inconceivable in the absence of an *English* 'component'. Regrettably, the Conservative-LibDem regime is based mainly upon street-walker conservatism – the new vendor on the block, wearing a new-new brand to reassure everyone the essence of the ancient statehood is safe, with a bit of goodwill. Some minor reforms are suggested, like Australian-style Alternative Vote, an elected Second Chamber, and enhanced 'local government' to divert popular energies and attention. The ship was badly holed, admittedly, after 13 years of 'New Labour' mediocrity and Gordon Brown's stalemate captaincy of 2008– 2010. However, sales staff can still argue that it's not yet doomed – provided that the new Cameron –Clegg administration shows itself to be one of adequate travelling repairs and replacement, guaranteed to restore seaworthiness *without English nationalism*.

Liberation from Pomland

I returned quite recently from some years in Melbourne, and, oddly enough, the programme may be more comprehensible from the Antipodean angle: what the 'Antipathies' have got round to perceiving is, approximately but rightly, the dying complex of attitudes identified in Australia as 'Pom' or 'Pommy'.[1] That is, 'English' not in the typically modern sense of ethnicity, language or genetic origins but in that of *superiority*, the inheritable (and probably eternal) distance of improved customs, outlook and exportability. This was an ideology naturally borne and transmitted by United Kingdom Empire and population transfer, over more than two centuries. Though comparable to other exports by competing powers like Spain, France, the Netherlands and Portugal, one need only list these to see an important difference. The English version has lasted much longer, without the defeats and other set-backs that were to affect its North-Atlantic neighbours. 'Anglo-Britishness' (as it might be more accurately titled) has survived remarkably intact, and since World War II even been reinforced by a curious 'special relationship' with the ascendant power of the United States. The Cold War refrigerator preserved it until the 1990s, and finally a 'New Labour' movement has carried it forward into another century.

Australians are familiar from recent experience with dubious right-of-centre coalitions. John Howard and the Liberal Party accomplished the trick over 11 years, via their alliance with the National Party (1996–2007). Yet that endured so long only because of a crucial factor that no longer applies, even in Great Britain. Wonderland characters like Cameron and Clegg may want it to be there at the end of Alice's fall; actually (as I suggested earlier) it has become another bit of Dodo nonsense. I refer to the mystique of capitalist growth-fetish known as 'Neo-Liberalism', the supposedly permanent exorcism from history of left-wing philosophies like socialism and equality. Howardite Liberalism flourished near the crest of the Neo-Liberal wave, in the '90s of last century. But Cameron-Cleggism has arrived far too late, and can only scrabble along in the ebbing tide. The only reason they aren't already washed into oblivion lies in the miserable oppositions they face: exhausted forms of post-Labour/Labor that spend decades over-ingratiating themselves into a supposed realism of pre-Crisis capitalist expansion. This is how the present battle of zombies was generated, claiming life-in-death in the name of one or other has-been creed.

A measure of nausea is surely in order here. England is failing to get its act together; but the resultant after-life of Britishness means all archipelago inhabitants are being sucked back into the graveyard, and (in effect) ordered to remain there. The peripheral populations mentioned above need the 'autonomy' (I would prefer to say, 'independence') to think differently, come to diverse conclusions, and invent a future going beyond the corsets of 'devolution'. Devolution was a recipe for forestalling and taming emergent political expression, by simultaneously conserving and re-imagining British-state traditions and culture. What it brought in the end was the present stalemate and incapacity. We're supposed to stay 'British', and thus go on sparing the English majority from undue self-appraisal and renewal. The basic instinct is that under Westminster 'democracy' could itself accomplish rebirth without the painful parturition of reforged national identity and self-discovery. 'Britain' has by self-definition stood above that 'sort of thing': it inherits 'bigger-than' by transmitted ectoplasmic continuity, the underlying spirit of imperial outreach and its successor, North-Atlantic Special-Relationism. We simply cannot break down into 'little' England, Scotland (and so forth) because the Great-Societal DNA rules it out: 'globalisation' has been turned into another form of such long-matured aspirations and delusions. Brit-chaps have to be dispensed from such backwardness (i.e. from demeaning connection to the origin of *homo sapiens* diversity and inescapable peculiarity).

The customs of Pom-land are deeply entrenched, and the Cameron–Clegg regime will try to revive them with the famous strategy from Count Lampedusa's extended-family novel *Il Gattopardo* (*The Leopard*, 1958): 'If we want things to stay as they are, things will have to change.' The true Sicily will never change – although its leopards and lions may have gone, to be replaced by jackals and hyenas, who think of themselves none the less as the salt of the earth. An earlier Labour Premier, Harold Wilson, once declared that Britain had to remain great or else be... '*nothing*'. Cautious electoral reforms will probably be undertaken to make the system seem 'fairer' – an Australian Alternative Vote rather than outright, all-round proportional representation. As for a Rudd-equivalent, the Labour Party was hard at work for some time trying to find one. Bizarrely enough, two of the contenders were the brothers David and Edward Miliband, sons of the late Ralph Miliband, the author of *Parliamentary Socialism: a Study of the Politics of Labour* (1961). This was a corrosive and unsparing analysis of the Labour Party, arguing that it had turned into a vehicle for the dilution or even outright betrayal of socialism. Miliband was a premature revolutionary, who saw Parliamenta*rism* as the formula that had changed the means into practically an end in itself: the corporate body of the Royal British state or 'Establishment', accepting both monarchy and the House of Lords as obligatory compromises along the road to power. Labourism had begun by colluding with Royal-British state-nationalism, and ended as another subject – even as its most enduring prop.

His sons reacted against fatherly dogma by joining the Labour Party, then trying to take it over. This is why I can't avoid a pressure of the heart today, imagining how he might feel on seeing one of them (Edward, the younger) victorious. Another exhumation of the corpse, reanimation by family blood. Will this never end? But of course the question in another sense suggests its own answer: it is only because the regime *is* ending that such spectacles are possible. How could the greatest of the later empires (and the closest to global authority) have gone quietly in the grey light of small-hour readjustment? The Ottomans and Austria– Hungary broke up into the Middle East and Balkan Europe, and the USSR into Russia and today's Central Asia; the least (and last) that Great Britain can do is face re-configuration of its archipelago into viable entities like 'Little England' (and the others). Such readjustment is already under way, and speeding up – and the surfacing of assorted nostalgics and romantic left-overs from the great story is a symptom of progress, unlikely to achieve more than moments of wallowing and regret.

Yet the problem of post-British readjustment is not in fact too daunting, by comparison with those others. One of its odd features is *relative* modernity: it rests in practice upon a political accord of the early 18th century, not a prehistoric popular fusion or conquest.

Great Britain's occupation of Ireland was certainly a specimen of the latter; but that was of course largely resolved in the 1920s, to leave behind only the somewhat distinct question of a partitioned, mainly Protestant Northern Ireland. The English conquest of Wales was also a 'typical' metropolitan take-over, or subjugation. None the less, the backbone of the United Kingdom has become the accord with the largest British-Isles minority, the Scots. And there was nothing typical about that. It was an early-modern political treaty between parliaments, confirming a joint monarchy and the prospective common endeavour of overseas expansion: the empire of the 18th to the 20th century. Revocation of such an agreement had been impossible within the former Westminster system, based on 1707s fusion of representative bodies; but of course this was replaced by the New Labour government's devolution of parliaments after 1998.

These reforms didn't shift the foundation of 'sovereignty'. They were designed to forestall any such change, after the rise of peripheral nationalisms during the last third of the 20th century. But such a reaffirmation of centrality could work only by acknowledging the emergent ground-plan. This was for a different kind of union, or association, among the various nations of 'those islands', naturally including England. *Scale* is secondary for such designs; but it was not allowed to appear so for a second by the unbending protagonists of 'Britishness'. To the latter, scale remains all: the standing of the UK first and foremost, as a world player rather than a 'nothing'; and after that (by implication) stress upon sufficient internal cohesion and assent, the social support-structure sustained by post–1707 over the mainland and as much as possible in post–1922 Ireland.

What such bombast both manifests and conceals is essentially the quandary of English national identity: compensation for occlusion by over-emphasis upon the most available 'imagined community' of the past, plus dread of 'little England'. Though exhibited in extreme ideological forms by the British National Party (BNP) and the anti-European United Kingdom Independence Party (UKIP), the emotional attitudes are widespread and comprehensible. Britishness was a strong drug, unavoidably fostered by many aspects of both the educational system and popular media culture, and also by today's weird combination of pro- and anti-Americanism. A popular monarchy also keeps it going – and lessens appetite for a specifically *English* contribution to the larger identity. Resentment of the Afghanistan involvement (for example) has become very widespread; but what Gordon Brown (and now his successors) count on is equally common acknowledgement of the special relationship, supposed to entail support of whatever *they* deem deeply significant.

What we are finding now is that such servitude is still preferred by most of the political ruling class to contraction: the dwindling echo of Greatness appeals more than any sobering admission of ordinary nationhood, and redefinition of the accompanying collective identity. Iraq didn't finish off the post-Great neurosis – will Afghanistan be more effective? Elections are due in Scotland and Wales in 2011, and for Alex Salmond's SNP government this is an opportunity to attempt a referendum on independence. Recent poll surveys indicate a majority still clinging to the Union, but the British parties will do all in their power to stop it happening: they know that a principle is at stake – the *right* of the smaller nations to decide on their future... and of course, behind that, the spectre of 'Little England' coming, at last, to claim *its* separate (shrunken) future as well.

It can be argued that Scotland, Wales and the North of Ireland have a duty to assert nationhood, not only for their own sake but for that of the English majority and (by close implication) that of the post-United Kingdom. No comprehensible new deal will be possible without the all-round re-formation of nationality politics; and Scotland is the key to this shift. David Cameron personally embodies deep-south Englishness, compelled to cover his restoration of Ukanian structures with an improbable alliance. Since Labourism has withdrawn from the scene, it can only be with what's left, the LibDem evocation of progressive Britannitude. The 'ConDem' coalition represents 'Not with a bang but a whimper', a half-hearted restoration of what in Australia continues to be labelled the 'Anglo–Celtic' heritage.

It is interesting to speculate on what difference the termination of this somewhat unnatural birthright could make. Though damaged, it weathered the nineteen-twenties loss of one part of Ireland. Is Anglo –Celticism long for this world; and what changes might its final collapse bring? Has Alice new, better discoveries to make down in the altered Wonderland where she's bound to end up?

Confederation?

Cameron's London coalition of 'ConDems' has given rise to a whole discourse of confidence-trickery and condemnation, the instinctive speech of zombieland. Aggravated by the analogy with 'condoms', it already makes it difficult to spell out the formula for post–2010 development in the post-United Kingdom. This can only be in the direction of *con*federation, and has been neatly expressed by Scottish commentator Gerry Hassan in a recent instalment of the *Open Democracy* web-site (www.open democracy.co.uk, 10 May):

> The familiar templates and landscape of the British political system is cracking and falling apart; the world of ... a two party adversarial system is no longer how our politics are shaped. In the last decade alone, the Conservative/Labour hold on our political system has vastly weakened and retreated, to a degree as yet not understood by the Westminster village. The 2010 election is further evidence of this, even if it is true the LibDems did not quite live up to the hype! Then there is also the evidence of the 'four nations' of the disunited kingdom, a state in the process of losing its over-arching United Kingdom politics, as we witness the emergence of four very different party systems across the UK.

This is why some confederal solution is becoming inevitable. Cameron's attempt to restore British unity is possible only via abandonment of two-party adversarial politics; but two-partyism was essential to the way that system worked – periods of consensus or

'National' government had always been temporary expedients intended to bring back normality. However, the 2010 crisis now looks like becoming permanent. The end of New Labour and the limits of Cameronian New Conservatism may at last usher in electoral and constitutional reform, going beyond the Alternative Vote. Unable to choose constitutional reform, the United Kingdom has fallen backwards into it – and in this tumble, one thing is bound to lead to another, with a more defined or 'little' England as one of the results. An Australian-style Federal answer is unlikely: the units are too unequal, and too socially distinct – as Labour's survival in Scotland, alongside nationalism, has vividly demonstrated.

The new regime 'Queen's Speech' has been broadcast while these last paragraphs were composed. This is the ritual whereby Her Majesty reads out the list of policy proposals given her by the Prime Minister she recently confirmed in office. The new forecast is for possible reforms of the voting system, most likely in two years time (once 'thoroughly debated' etc.). Given the sloth of Commons procedures, plus the opposition of many Conservatives to any change whatever, all one can say is that an 'Australian' order *might* then arise in the homeland. Alternative Vote could be chosen as a safer alternative to proportional representation, conserving two-partyism in a more presentable fashion and allowing a fairer system for any Second Chamber replacing the House of Lords. But one may reasonably doubt whether this will be in time. In a world where, as the authors of a recent study of Indian nationalism point out: 'There are at least 2,500 potential nationalities in the world waiting to stake their claim to full nationhood', it appears unlikely that the populations of Wales and Scotland will wait patiently for future reassignment.[2] At this moment, 2011 looks the most likely date for serious re-commencement of the Scottish independence initiative, very likely to be followed by that of Wales. If the existing Westminster coalition government endures, and whether or not its half-hearted constitutional reforms reach the statute book, then breaking-up (or a reconstitution) process will take its course. In 1977 I thought of that as 'The Break-up of Britain', and in 2000 took the argument farther with *After Britain: New Labour and the Return of Scotland* (Verso Books). Today I see no reason for regretting, or revising these titles.

Notes

1   The title probably derives from the name of a ship, the Pommern, which sailed regularly to Melbourne in the later 19th century. Of Baltic origins ('Pomerania') it carried a superior class of immigrant from the Thames Estuary, those able to afford the accomodation. Though 'Pommies' were originally passengers disembarking from this ship, the term didn't become generally used until the 1920s, after World War 1 – probably via experience of the English officer corps in the Middle East and France. With time, what was a social class label became 'ethnic', in the sense of applying to anyone from England.

2   *Creating a Nationality: the Ramjanmhabumi Movement and fear of the Self*, by Ashish Nandy and others, Oxford India Paperbacks, 1997; Preface p.xi.

CHAPTER 5

The Fish, the Ferry and the Black Crude Reality

NEIL KAY

THE 1973 PLAY *The Cheviot, the Stag and the Black, Black Oil* by John McGrath was a phenomenon that was very much of its time. It mixed rising nationalist sentiment and a growing consciousness of the prospects that oil could hold for economic independence with what was left over from the '60s desire for radical reform. At least it did for me, just about on my way to my first job as a professional economist, with my rising nationalist sentiment and my residual radicalism left over from a '60s student lifestyle.

That play reflected the politics of socialism, itself a distinguished and well established tradition in Scotland, but it also reflected the politics of grievance, equally well established, but much less distinguished. After the sound and fury of the performance it left the question; 'well… what are you going to do about it?'

I also remember from the following year the American reporter from *Time* magazine who had been touring Scotland in a taxi looking for stories on 'resurgent nationalism', and who was now homing in on Stirling University as a well known hotbed of rabid revolutionaries. But he found 'no demonstrations, no underground armies of the night, no threats of violence in the air'[1], which, while reassuring for the cause of stable governance, did not make for great copy. I had seen McGrath's play the previous year, and while I cannot remember whether my answer was influenced by that experience, I do remember the reporter pressing us hard on why we did not want to take government by storm. As *Time* magazine reported in April 1974:

> 'You can't live day to day with your own rage,' says Neil Kay,
> 25, a graduate student in economics at Stirling University and
> a Nationalist activist. 'If we're going to do anything, we are
> going to do it by rational and reasonable methods.'[2]

In my defence, I was in the process of transmuting to nationalism
after a long sojourn in the Liberal Party, and had just spent seven
years studying economics at undergraduate and postgraduate level. If
by then you had not accepted the basic economic premise that all
individuals are rational decision-makers, you would have quickly
found out you had no future in the economics profession. But
'Independence by all rational and reasonable methods' does not a
stirring call to action make, especially when uttered in the shade of
the Wallace Monument, just a few miles from Bannockburn.

Now 34 years on, after numerous encounters with politicians, but
particularly with civil servants (for whom Dante might reasonably
have dedicated a special Circle), I am not so convinced now as I was
then that rational reasonable argument may be sufficient. I am also
less convinced than I was then that some occasional rage (non-violent,
properly channelled) would necessarily be a bad thing.

If my views have evolved over the years, then much the same could
be said of economics. Economics today has largely recognised and
even tentatively embraced concepts such as irrationality, ignorance and
other aspects reflecting the contrariness and fallibility of human nature.
At the same time, I cannot completely forswear the default working
premise that I have inherited down the years as an economist which I
might express now as: when all else fails, fall back on rational, reasonable argument.

After several decades of arguments and debates on the economics
of Scottish independence with sceptics, I find that issues can be
sharpened and clarified by ignoring the Scottish case to begin with
and asking the sceptic just two questions. Question (a) do you believe
that separate countries should exist? If the sceptic answers in the
negative, there is no point in proceeding any further. But if, as most

do, they answer in the positive (albeit reluctantly in some cases) then you proceed to the second question. Question (b) what principles should determine the boundaries of countries?

At that point you can have a useful discussion about the role of shared or distinctive legal, political, historical, cultural institutions in creating sensible principles for setting the boundaries of nations, always subject to the popular will, while citing cases to illustrate the point. At some stage the sceptic will usually sense which way the wind is blowing as far as the case for Scottish independence is concerned. What I find is that many will attempt to pre-empt this by arguing that even if there was a case for Scottish independence, actually getting there would be too painful or too costly. In short, they will implicitly argue that the temporary process and costs of transition would trump any subsequent long term gains that could be achieved under independence itself.

One of the most quoted phrases in economics is John Maynard Keynes's: 'In the long run we are all dead'[3]. Some sceptics, particularly those with a background in economics, are prone to quote Keynes at this point as an effective rebuttal of the case for the long term benefits of an independent Scotland. Concentrate on the here and now, they will argue, avoid the costs and distraction of a painful separation and an uncertain future.

What is less well known than Keynes's aphorism is the sentence that preceded it; 'Long run is a misleading guide to current affairs'[4]. That is the context in which he was arguing and it is as true today as it was in 1923. The long term forecasts for the global economy in 10 years time are not much help to the Monetary Policy Committee when it has to set interest rates today. But that does not mean that sensible action today cannot be taken with a view to influencing events well beyond the short term horizon, otherwise none of us would take out a 20-year mortgage, buy insurance, or even educate our children. Keynes himself was very much aware of the interconnectedness between the present and the future, as would be expected from one who essayed on 'economic possibilities for our grandchildren'[5]. The problem with

Keynes' aphorism regarding mortality and the long run is that when it is quoted out of context it can mesh well with, and help justify, political short-termism and natural instincts towards small 'c' conservatism, apathy, and inertia.

We take here as given that the current boundaries of Scotland would represent a sensible basis around which to constitute an independent country; the legal, political, historical, cultural justification for this has been made many times before, and will be made many times again, leaving the only issue to be settled that of the popular will. What I want to concentrate on is the question of alternatives, and to short cut the discussion I will focus on what are the only two likely alternatives, the status quo (albeit with some further minor devolution of powers) and independence within Europe. Even moderate reform of the status quo would quickly come up against such issues as the Barnett Formula[6], the West Lothian Question[7], fiscal autonomy, and the issue of oil funds. It is difficult to conceive of any package of constitutional reforms that could deliver a stable outcome (holding measures such as the Calman Commission[8] notwithstanding), bearing in mind that they would have to achieve a political consensus on both sides of the border. As for independence, it is also assumed that this means independence within the EC, there being little evidence of political or popular will for any alternative to Community membership.

A Union Dividend?

Is there a 'Union Dividend' for Scotland from continuing with the UK? In 2006, the then First Minister Jack McConnell said in a speech;

> We all benefit from a Union dividend and all that it secures –
> the free movement of citizens, the increase in trade and oppor-
> tunities for our businesses and the sharing of values and
> aspirations[9].

But is that it? After 300 years, one would hope for a little more substance in defence of the Union. The first two items on this very short list (free movement of citizens, increase in trade and opportunities for business) are now delivered as a matter of statutory obligation and rote though membership of a wider union within Europe, rendering UK union membership redundant in these respects. Probing these items reveals them to be little more than versions of the 'access to Empire markets' which passed their sell-by date many years ago.

Even when it might have had arguable validity, the 'access to Empire' argument was actually a form of political protection racket to the effect that you would be given reason to be sorry if you did not join our Empire-ya-bas gang. It is irrelevant today in the context of a globalised market and a European Union.

As for the idea that maintenance of the Union is necessary for 'sharing of values and aspirations', it is difficult to see how Irish independence has impeded healthy cross-fertilisation of ideas and cultures back and forth across the Irish sea, and it is equally difficult to see how and why that would or should happen in the case of Scottish independence.

A 'family ties' version of the 'sharing of values and aspirations' argument was recently put forward by Gordon Brown when he promoted a Fabian pamphlet[10] he co-authored with Douglas Alexander. The UK Prime Minister said the pamphlet would make the '21st century case for the Union', and that case would be built on family ties. 'When the Act of Union was signed, only 30,000 Scots had English relatives, and now the figure is 2.5 million,' Mr Brown said. 'It will seem strange to consider breaking a union when 2.5 million Scots have strong ties, family ties, with England.'[11].

But it did not seem strange to the citizenry of the United States in 1776, in their own Declaration of Independence when they declaimed: 'Nor have we been wanting in attentions to our British brethren... we have conjured [sic] them by the ties of our common kindred... They too have been deaf to the voice of justice and of consanguinity'[12].

In fact, 'family ties' do not have a very convincing or respectable track record in debates about independence, whether it is the white

Rhodesians 'having demonstrated loyalty to the Crown and to their kith and kin in the United Kingdom and elsewhere', as they made clear in their Unilateral Declaration of Independence[13], to the old Soviet argument about not giving the Baltic states independence because so many Russian citizens lived there.

Indeed, a counter argument could be made that, rather than facilitating the 'sharing' of values and aspiration, the Union has led to undue and unhealthy homogenisation, with the dominant partner in this Union dictating the terms. Like many of my baby boomer generation growing up in Scotland, I was taught that if you were reasonably clever, you did languages, if you were fairly clever you did Latin, and if you were really clever you did Latin *and* Greek. I have no recollection of anyone ever telling us why that was the case, I had to work it out later for myself. In fact, a knowledge of classics was a prerequisite for an Oxbridge education, indeed Latin had been a required subject for applicants to Oxford and Cambridge until the 1960s. If you wanted an exemplar from the education sphere of the 'sharing of values and aspirations' that was part and parcel of the Union dividend, then Oxbridge was it.

Of course, Latin and Greek can be interesting and stimulating intellectual disciplines but the crucial economic notion here is that of opportunity cost, or the value of the alternatives which might have been pursued instead of the chosen activity. As with any rating or rankings system, if something is prized highly, the corollary is that other things are not so highly valued. If you were not so clever, it was made very clear to you that your future was more likely to lie with the technical and engineering subjects.

At the very time in history when Scotland should have been con-solidating and building on its status as 'the World's Workshop' in Tom Devine's graphic phrase[14], we were teaching our children that the pinnacle of intellectual excellence lay in knowing the difference between ablative absolutes and subordinate relative clauses in long dead foreign languages, benchmarked as preparation for an entrance exam they would never sit, for an Oxbridge university that would not want them, and to which they would probably not wish to go even if the opportunity arose.

If one image could serve as a metaphor for Scotland's 20th century industrial decline, it would be serried ranks of redundant cranes along the Clyde and serried ranks of children in classrooms across Scotland chanting 'amo, amas, amat'. This would also serve as an endnote to one of the most remarkable stories of industrial power and influence wielded from a population base that was still less than five million by the end of its peak.

This phenomenon is described in detail by Tom Devine[15]. He narrates how Scotland advanced from a relatively low industrial base around 1830 to a position of global dominance in several key sectors in a few decades: 'coal, iron, steel, shipbuilding and engineering took off and transformed Scotland into a manufacturer for the world'[16]. At one point, Coats of Paisley controlled 80 per cent of global thread-making capacity. At the time of World War 1, Scotland had built about one-fifth of the world's shipping tonnage then in use. 'At the heart of the heavy industrial complex with its world-wide markets was the huge range of engineering specialisms in engine pumps, hydraulic equipment, railway rolling stock and a host of other products'[17].

It was not just the sheer scale of industrialisation and emergent Scottish industrial power and prestige that had been so impressive from the early 19th century onwards, it was the impetus provided by Scottish technological developments. Devine notes[18] that a primary factor in Scotland's transformation was a remarkable rate of strategic invention and innovation in metal working and ship construction, and the story of rapid technological progress added to other sectors in this rich industrial broth.

The final element in this transformation was the interdependencies and technological spillovers between industries and sectors. 'It was perhaps almost inevitable that from this great congeries of skills in precision engineering would come an interest in the application of steam propulsion to ships'[19]; 'the fortunes of shipbuilding, iron and steel became very closely linked'[20]. Devine also observes that Scotland's industrial base in textiles (which actually pre-dated the first Industrial Revolution) also played an important role as a catalyst for later developments in shipbuilding[21].

What Devine, the historian, is describing is what would be described by economists as an industrial cluster[22]. Industrial clusters vary in character and significance, they may be seen at the level of a city or geographical region (Silicon Valley; Detroit – 'Motor City') or even a city district (Hollywood; City of London). What we know from the work of Michael Porter[23] and others about robust and healthy industrial clusters is that they tend to be highly geographically concentrated but internationally oriented, involve networks of firms up and down supply chains, and have strong links (competitive and co-operative) at various stages within a particular industrial sector, and between firms in related sectors. It can also involve links with institutions outside the industrial sector such as universities and other sources of innovative and technical knowledge.

All of these elements were present in the creation of Silicon Valley. You can trace back the genesis of many of the companies that were to become major world players to spinoffs from Hewlett-Packard. In turn, Hewlett-Packard was the brainchild of the eponymous students who were mentored and supported by Frederick Terman, professor of electrical engineering at Stanford University. It has been said that if Hewlett and Packard were the fathers of Silicon Valley, then their teacher Frederick Terman was the grandfather.

What is also known is that there are certain conditions which are not highly conducive to cluster formation, such as stand-alone one-off entrepreneurs, concentration at limited stages of the supply chain such as production of raw materials or serving the final consumers, and a branch factory heritage which tends not to have the in-house scientific and technical expertise in branches that help spawn spin-offs. Silicon Valley in California is a healthy industrial cluster, the same could not have been said of Silicon Glen in Scotland.

There is a limit to what a government can do to encourage cluster formation, if they have a role it is more like a midwife than a parent, and just as with babies it can take a long time for clusters to grow up – typically much longer than the length of a single parliamentary term. These days, Keynes might have said; 'in the long run we just might have a viable industrial cluster'. It does take a kind of self-denying vision for politicians – and development agencies – to take the steps now that will allow their successors to reap the rewards in the future, a kind of vision that certainly politicians are not renowned for in the absence of conditions of war or depression.

These are not radical ideas, they are well established, and indeed Porter's clusters framework was adopted as policy framework by the government's development agency Scottish Enterprise in the late '90s with a number of analysts[24] providing key insights and advice as to how the framework could be applied in a Scottish context.

Scottish Enterprise certainly knows the right things and has been doing the right things, but they are essentially a facilitator and it is the fate of a facilitator to be held responsible for failure and to find the glory for any success to be appropriated by others, perhaps years down the line. That does not mean that its performance in executing a clusters strategy has been either good or bad, what it means is that if Scottish Enterprise did not exist, something like it and its clusters policy would have to be invented. What we want to know, is how effective would such strategies be in the context of Scotland's membership of the Union. The answer to that question may be found, at least in part, by considering why one of the most remarkable industrial clusters in modern industrial history unravelled so quickly and so thoroughly. Why was Scotland's 19th century industrial hegemony usurped so comprehensively in the 20th century?

Sharing values and aspirations

A simplistic answer to the question just posed would be that it was not surprising that what went up with the growth of Empire also went down with it, and that is an answer which has some attractions particularly for those who find some aspects of Scotland's association with militaristic empire-building distasteful. Certainly there is a broad coincidence of timing and it provides for a neat explanation along with other associated facts and influences such as exhaustion of raw materials, over-dependence on heavy industry, union-management relations, emergence of new low-cost competitors, and so on

But I think that the 'decline of Empire' answer is too easy, though it does add further emphasis to the irrelevance of any modern variant on the 'access to Empire' argument for keeping the Union. If we accept that Scotland hitched a very productive ride on the back of Empire, it still does not really explain why Scotland's subsequent industrial decline from its Victorian peaks was so precipitate and emphatic. Hitching rides gets you further down the road compared to those still left thumbing a lift. By the start of the 20th century, Scotland actually had quite a diversified industrial base, it had tremendous scientific and engineering resources, not just in its industrial enterprises but in its universities, and it had a well deserved international reputation for entrepreneurship, not just earned from its home-made Victorian heritage but in markets across the world. With that start in 20th century life that most countries of equivalent size would happily have swapped their own resource endowments for, how could things have gone so badly wrong?

Paradoxically, the eventual weakening of Scotland's industrial position as part of the Union might best be illustrated by examining some of its vaunted strengths. Duncan Bannatyne is a very successful self-made Scottish entrepreneur who built up a £200m chain of health clubs, but is now perhaps best known for his panel membership of the television programme *Dragons' Den* which focuses on seeking out new entrepreneurial talent. He recently argued:

> There are some phenomenal Scottish entrepreneurs, I could name so many. There's Sir Tom Hunter, Brian Souter, Sir Tom Farmer, you could go on and on. The spirit of Scottish enterprise goes back hundreds of years. Adam Smith explained markets and free enterprise, Robert Dunlop brought us Dunlop tyres,

John Logie Baird brought us TV, Alexander Bell gave us the telephone, John McAdam gave us Tarmac. It was even a Scot, William Paterson, who founded the Bank of England.[25]

As far as the historical cases are concerned, if we first remove Adam Smith (who observed and documented entrepreneurship rather than practised it himself), then the single most obvious feature joining together Dunlop, Baird, Bell, McAdam and Paterson is that they all became successful after having first left Scotland. Whether that says more about the qualities of the individuals themselves, or the economic and social context they left behind, is an open question. What can be said is that the mere act of leaving your native country and having to survive without a supportive but stifling 'ah kent yer faither' social network can often be the catalyst for entrepreneurial activity. The migrant plucked from social roots can have a stronger private need for success and face less social opprobrium for failure than had they stayed home. When I grew up in Fraserburgh my newsagent was Dyga, my first (summer) job was with Borowski the photographer and had I stayed on long enough to buy my first car it would probably have been from Shrader down the road. The unifying factor underlying these three businesses is that they were all started by enterprising Polish immigrants, servicemen who had stayed on after the end of World War II. It is important to us that Andrew Carnegie was a Scot, but perhaps equally or even more important was his familial background as economic migrants. As far as the contemporary examples of successful entrepreneurship that Bannatyne gives are concerned, Brian Souter who founded Stagecoach, Sir Tom Farmer who founded Kwik Fit and Sir Tom Hunter who founded Sports Division are all frequently cited (often in the same breath) as exemplifying successful self-made Scottish entrepreneurship. There is absolutely no doubt they do represent exactly that, and individually and together represent superb examples of entrepreneurial activity of the highest quality. But each of them represent thin slivers of economic activity right at the end of the supply chain where it meets the final consumer. Who designed, developed and made the coaches that Stagecoach drives, the automotive components that Kwik Fit fits, the sports shoes that Sports Division sells, and the equipment that Duncan Bannatyne's health clubs use? The relevant part of the answer to each question is that it was not Scotland. As in the Sherlock Holmes story of the dog that did not bark[26], here there are several dogs that did not bark. Successful Scottish migrant entrepreneurs are one thing, but why do their reputations and performance in Scotland's story seem to overshadow those who stayed at home? Where were they all? Selling services to the final consumer in clubs, shops and buses (and, we might add through financial and tourist services) genuinely adds value, but why has Scotland not also retained or created strong presences further back up the supply chain to root these end-activities in the high value-added stages and increase the chances of creating sustainable competitive advantage that will outlive the careers of individual entrepreneurs?

This is not in any way to belittle the achievements of the seriously impressive contemporary entrepreneurs listed by (and including) Bannatyne, but it does raise questions regarding sustainable competitive advantage. It is true that Scotland is not alone amongst Western countries in going through what has been termed de-industrialisation, with service sector industries displacing manufacturing over whole swathes of the economy. Much of that is part of a natural, inevitable and indeed positive evolutionary process. But where you find modern international competitive advantage it tends not to be embodied in hero-entrepreneur figures like Alan Sugar and Donald Trump, beloved though they may be of reality TV series on both sides of the Atlantic. Instead, international competitive advantage comes in clusters of inter-related entrepreneurial activity, and whatever might be said about the excellent qualities of Souter, Farmer, Hunter and Bannatyne, membership of, or association with, a discernable industrial cluster is not one of them. I want to be clear that I am not suggesting that Scotland's industrial decline was precipitated by an unhealthy obsession with classical declensions and conjugations, to do so would be to confuse symptoms with causes. But to the extent that the final item of the Union dividend set out above by the former First Minister is concerned, 'the sharing of values and aspirations' is not one that I regard as having, on balance having had a beneficial effect on Scotland's economic performance, and try as I might, I have never found a useful application for the fact that I know that the Latin for table is 'mensa'. The most productive thing I did in Latin was to prove deficient[27] in the area of conjugations and declensions, which resulted in my banishment to engineering. The skills I subsequently learned in engineering draughtsmanship proved unexpectedly useful some decades later when I was able draw on them in using computer graphics programmes in my own economics research[28].

Much has been written[29] about Scottish education including the influence of what I would describe as Oxbridge standards but to an economist, it all comes back to opportunity cost. Again, if you make one thing a priority, you downgrade something else, and the set of values and aspirations that have been downgraded and degraded over the last century has been Scotland's engineering and scientific heritage. If this seems philistine, the contribution that liberal arts make to social and cultural life is fully acknowledged, but they should be complementary to a healthy respect for the engineering sciences, not a substitute for them. As with most things, it is a matter of emphasis and balance, and the Union heritage here has been seriously imbalanced. I think that if Scottish values and aspirations had not been overlain and crowded out by Southern values that the name of the former Chancellor of Dundee University (1992–2006) would be regarded by many as candidate for greatest living Scot. He is certainly one of the most remarkable Scots of all time. Amongst other work he developed beta blockers and helped revolutionise heart treatment. The commercial value of the scientific work he produced could probably buy and sell the assets of an entire Dragons' Den several times over. He was awarded the Nobel Prize for Medicine in 1988. And if you have not heard of him recently, or do not even know who he is[30], that rather makes my point.

Fish, Ferries and Black Crude Realities

So where do the fish, the ferry, and the black crude reality come into all this? In some respects, as for nationalist sentiments generally, it is grounded in personal experience, but they each are also indicative of fault lines in terms of the relations between Scotland and the rest of the UK. In the part of Scotland where I grew up, just about everybody's livelihood was directly or indirectly dependent on the fish. And where I live now, just about everybody's livelihood is directly or indirectly dependent on the ferries. Such dependency is echoed up and down the North and West coasts of Scotland. The black crude reality is of course the black crude oil that has become the dominant economic activity over much of the North-East of Scotland where I come from. None of this is surprising, much of what Scotland has become today reflects the sea, most obviously from our history as a trading nation and the undersea resources around our coasts, but also in terms of the differing influences of what were proximate cultures and economies around the Scottish coast, whether west, north or east. They also have all one thing in common. These are all significant resources in a Scottish context where many livelihoods and communities depend on them. But as far as the rest of the UK is concerned, if all the fish, the ferries and the black crude oil disappeared overnight this would have relatively little impact on UK economies and societies outwith Scotland, though the Isle of Wight might feel the same pain as Mull if the ferries disappeared, while the Treasury would find it had a black hole where once there was black gold. As far as the fish is concerned, in 2006, just three ports of Peterhead, Lerwick and Fraserburgh accounted for 49 per cent by quantity and 36 per cent by value of all landings by UK vessels into the UK[31]. While there are other localised pockets of activity outside Scotland within the UK, in relative terms the fishing industry simply does not have the same importance in the rest of the UK as it does in Scotland. Where this matters is in terms of political agendas and priorities. Within the EU, Scottish fishing policy is a UK responsibility despite the fact that it is less relevant at that level than it is in Scotland. As far as ferries are concerned, I have given invited evidence to three different Inquiries set up by the Scottish Parliament's Transport Committees (2001, 2005 and 2008). But any pretence that Scottish ministers over the years might have wished to communicate that they were somehow in control of ferry policy (for reason of vanity, credibility or whatever) was essentially a sham. When Brussels writes about policy issues concerning CalMac or Northlink ferries, they do not write to the Scottish Transport Minister or even the First Minister. They write to the UK Foreign Minister, because that is where real power and responsibility lies. And that in turn brings us to the crude reality, the issue of the oil.

Over the last few years, evidence has been accumulating that Scotland has been performing poorly judged against international comparators (including UK) in terms of growth, levels of new business formation and sluggish productivity, including the phenomenon of declining Scottish tax revenue from various sources as share of UK tax revenue[32]. At first sight this seems puzzling; after all has not Scotland had the benefit of a tremendous windfall boost to its growth opportunities with the injections of North Sea oil into the equation in recent years? Should it not be accelerating past (at the very least) its Southern neighbour rather than appearing to be falling further behind on a number of growth-related indicators?

I looked at this issue in 2007 when as one of a panel of economists I submitted invited evidence to the Scottish Parliament's Finance Committee as part of its Inquiry into the Scottish Executive's statistical series *Government Expenditure and Revenue in Scotland*. What I found was remarkable for a number of reasons, but particularly for one crucial and central fact. Scotland's slow growth was not puzzling in the face of the North Sea oil bonanza, on the contrary it is exactly what should have been expected for any country or region which has been blessed (or cursed) with an abundance of natural resources.

The phenomenon is called the 'Resource Curse', which, even though it has strong support from empirical evidence[33], has only become widely acknowledged in the last few years. Contrary to what might be expected, countries and regions which have an abundance of natural resources (such as oil) tend to have slower growth than countries and regions which do not possess these natural assets – there is, it appears, a 'Resource Curse'. A number of possible reasons for the Resource Curse have been suggested, but one set of particular relevance to Scotland was identified by the Harvard economists Sachs and Warner[34]. They found that the demand for basic inputs (e.g. land and labour) from the natural resource sector could drive up input costs, squeezing the profits (and crowding out) internationally traded activities such as manufacturing that compete with the natural resource sector for these same inputs.

Once manufacturing has been crowded out, the brakes are put on the growth process. While the Resource Curse has been most convincingly documented at country level, recent work is now suggesting that it can hold at the level of a resource-abundant region within a developed country[35], which is of course the position that Scotland finds itself in.

As I noted in my evidence to the Finance Committee, an economist from Mars, knowing all about the Resource Curse but nothing about Scotland, would not be surprised by news of the poor performance of the Scottish economy and its contingent tax revenues following the windfall of North Sea oil.

However, that is not the end of the bad news for Scotland as part of the Union. I noted in my evidence to the Finance Committee that Scotland could be doubly cursed in the absence of specific policies framed to counter a Resource Curse, the first curse (the Resource Curse itself) during the extraction phase, the second curse that of being left competitively disadvantaged with weakened tradable sectors once the oil eventually does runs out. Solution? A thoughtful – and independent – country such as Norway sets up an oil fund to help plug the gaps and create the growth opportunities that will be needed once the oil runs out. An oil fund might not guarantee happiness but it could at least provide an insurance policy against misery. To just use the oil for current consumption is eating the seed corn. But the chances of Scotland being able to negotiate its own oil fund within the Union (which even states or provinces like Alaska and Alberta have been able to do) is politically improbable given growing popular opinion outside Scotland that it is already overcompensated for through the Barnett Formula.

In some respects the arguments about the Resource Curse seem to have similarities with arguments that Scotland's public sector spending and employment have crowded out private sector activity. In fact, the crowding out argument is more about the performance of the economy, while the Resource Curse argument is about the structure of the economy. No matter how the economy is governed, we will still need police, firemen, doctors and nurses. After that, questions revolve around how well such services are organised and managed. And as far as wealth creation is concerned, a good teacher can have a long term, permanent and economy-wide effect that can outstrip many an entrepreneur, as the example of Frederick Terman demonstrates spectacularly.

Conclusions

If we did not already have a Union, few today would suggest forming it. In terms of fit between the institutions, traditions, economies, and cultures of the two countries it makes about as much sense as a Sweden/ Denmark amalgamation or a France/ Netherlands merger. So why does it still persist? A shrewd political observer once wrote a treatise on how to obtain and keep political power. In it he noted:

> ...there is nothing more difficult to take in hand, more perilous to conduct, or more uncertain in its success, than to take the lead in the introduction of a new order of things. Because the innovator has for enemies all those who have done well under the old conditions, and lukewarm defenders in those who may do well under the new. This coolness arises partly from fear of the opponents, who have the laws on their side, and partly

from the incredulity of men, who do not readily believe in new things until they have had a long experience of them. Thus it happens that whenever those who are hostile have the opportunity to attack they do it like partisans, whilst the others defend lukewarmly.[36]

For 'the innovator' in the above quote read 'independence'. Fear, fostering of doubt and sense of inferiority, dark warnings not to risk what we have, short-termism, advocacy of the status quo – the defenders of the Union may not all have read Machiavelli's *The Prince*, but many of them behave as if they have. It is easier to scaremonger about things that exist than to guarantee what might be. But if we just exist, and simply ignore what might be, events will shape us when it is we who should be shaping events. There must be a more optimistic future for Scotland than that.

We need to drive further back up the supply chain because that is where the value is ultimately generated, more towards what Casson calls high level entrepreneurship involving major technological innovation, which he distinguishes from entrepreneurship based on market trading or shopkeeping[37]. Is the Union the best vehicle to pursue such an effort? Judging by the evidence, I would say not. Much of Scotland's innovative potential has been hollowed out over the years and if there was one crucial, defining error that could be said to be at the root of Scottish industrial 20th century decline, it was the Union 'dividend' of believing that 'technical' subjects were automatically and necessarily intellectually inferior to more 'academic' subjects such as the classics. To think we were all taught such utter nonsense! Try telling that to the engineers of Silicon Valley or the graduates of India's technical institutes. If America had never won its independence, the equivalent of Frederick Terman teaching in the equivalent of Stanford University would probably have been a professor of classics, while the equivalents of Hewlett and Packard could well have finished up teaching Latin and Greek at some obscure Midwestern finishing school for the sons and daughters of ranching gentlefolk.

Now, 34 years on, there are some striking similarities, but some differences, from the time that reporter interviewed that young economics student about the imminence of independence. There is again strong interest in Scottish independence, Labour is both in power and in trouble at UK level, oil is back on the agenda with a vengeance, and there is a resurgent SNP.

Differences include the fact that we have, of course, the re-creation of the Scottish Parliament which, despite some prognostications, has failed to kill Scottish independence stone dead. As far as the oil is concerned, the difference now is to be found in the basic economic lesson that when something becomes scarcer, it becomes more valuable. There may be less oil in the ground in future years, but what there is will be worth more. But the Resource Curse and the follow on consequences mean Scotland will be doubly cursed if we stay part of the Union and the North Sea continues to be treated as the Treasury's piggy bank.

Despite all that has been said here, there are grounds for hope. Scottish Enterprise's priority industries of life sciences, energy, financial markets, electronics markets are particularly suited to a clusters perspective and even the other more traditional priority industries of tourism, food and drink are ones in which Scotland has a comparative advantage. But promoting these in a Union context in many respects goes against the grain of a governance culture and philosophy which can prize a liberal arts education more highly than an engineering background. We need to get back to where we came from, which is a respect for the continuity of hands-on technical excellence and scientific brilliance that runs all the way from James Watt to James Black (you knew who he was all along, didn't you?). It is time to bring responsibility, accountability, power and control back home where it belongs, not just for the fish, the ferries, and the oil, but for all these things that impinge directly on Scottish culture, economics, politics, technology and society.

These arguments transcend narrow issues of productivity and economic growth, and impact on broader issues of social values.

Should the provision of ferry services be seen as having social implications justifying subsidy, or should they be left for the market to
provide? What should be the main driver underlying the provision of
school education – high quality education for all pupils or parental
choice? Should elimination of unemployment be a priority for a government, or should it simply be one of several objectives alongside
control of inflation and pursuit of growth?

While economics can help look at the implications of different
answers to these questions, the answers themselves ultimately depend
on social and cultural values, which in turn can be contingent on
time and place. Clearly there can be widely divergent answers to
these questions even within countries, but for our purposes the
crucial point is that the consensus view in each case can differ
markedly between countries. This in turn can – and should – influence
political choices.

This is uncontroversial and only becomes an issue when political
choices for different countries are subsumed and constrained within
a unitary state. Devolution has already begun to highlight possible
fault lines where social and cultural values may differ (or at least
have a differing emphasis) between Scotland and England. Should
England, like Scotland, abolish bridge tolls, have free care for the
elderly, and end prescription charges? There is no law, economic or
otherwise, that says they should; equally there is no law that says
they should not. The question is about political choices, which in
turn are influenced by what the consensus in a country thinks should
be priorities. Devolution has already gone some way to freeing up
political choices that reflect legitimate differences in social and
cultural values – or priorities – between Scotland and England. But
devolution is only a half way house, what both Scotland and the rest
of the UK need is the ability to take independent decisions sensitive to
the particular values that the unitary state simply wallpapers over.

In the words of my *alma mater*, Fraserburgh Academy's motto,
'*Sapientia Clavis Vitae*' ('Wisdom is the key of life', dummy), As for
the rest, *carpe diem*. The Greeks may have had a word for it, but I

confess the Romans could still turn a good phrase. And it beats 'independence by all rational and reasonable methods' hands down. QED[38]

Addendum

Much has happened in the 2–3 years since this chapter was written and a great deal of it has served to illuminate and reinforce the arguments of that earlier work. In one sense the near collapse of whole swathes of the Scottish financial sector reinforced my earlier points about the morphing of Scottish industry into a nation of shop-keepers and market traders. But surely at another level this showed up the weakness of traditional Scottish values in this crucial sector, and also our luck that there was a big brother out there at UK level to bail us out?

On the contrary, the financial crisis and particularly the fate of RBS and Bank of Scotland are the most extreme examples possible of my argument that sharing 'values and aspirations' with our dominant neighbour to the south has been to the detriment of Scottish interests and the economic and social development of the country.

The First Minister Alex Salmond (one of Scotland's most able and influential economists) recently recounted to me how he had worked in one of Scotland's leading banks in the early 1980s and had seen how hire purchase companies had been obtaining interest rates on their loans far in excess of those achieved by the bank on its loans. He lobbied his boss; was this not a high return business that the bank itself should have an interest in? Would not competition help both bank and consumer alike?

In the banking culture that emerged out of the Thatcherite 'get-rich-quick, tell-Sid, treat-them-as-mugs' mentality, even by the '80s such advice would have been regarded as laughably conservative. But this was before all that. The boss of the young Salmond rose to his feet, walked around his desk a couple of times, then fixed his young protégé with a steely eye and hissed;

'Do you **know** what you are proposing? Usury, young man, Usury'...

After that, the traditional Scottish reputation for caution, trust and responsibility in financial services that had taken generations to build up took less than a few years to first be exploited, then explode. Sharing of values and aspirations? Oh yes, that has got us where we are today all right.

Notes

1   McWhirter, W. (1974) *When the Black Rain Falls, Time Magazine*, 8 April http://www.time.com/time/magazine/article/0,9171,908536,00.html

2   Ibid

3   Keynes, J. M. (1924) *A Tract on Monetary Reform*, London Macmillan, ch.3

4   Ibid

5   Keynes, J. M. (1963) Economic Possibilities for our Grandchildren, in, *Essays in Persuasion*, New York: W. W. Norton & Co., pp. 358–373 (essay originally published in 1930)

6   Kay, N. M. (2002) The Barnett formula and the Squeeze, in, Calling Scotland to Account, Policy Institute, pp.44–49

7   During a 1977 debate on Scottish and Welsh devolution, Tam Dalyell, MP for West Lothian, asked, 'For how long will English constituencies and English Honourable members tolerate... at least 119 Honourable Members from Scotland, Wales and Northern Ireland exercising an important, and probably often decisive, effect on British politics while they themselves have no say in the same matters in Scotland, Wales and Northern Ireland?' He offered his own potential situation as an example: as an MP he would be able to vote on matters affecting Blackburn, Lancashire, but not of Blackburn, West Lothian in his own constituency.

8   Commission on Scottish Devolution 2008–09, Chaired by Sir Kenneth Calman

9   Speech by Rt. Hon. Jack McConnell MSP First Minister of Scotland 10 November 2006, IPPR http://www.ippr.org.uk/uploadedFiles/events/Jack McConnell_10.11.06.pdf

10 Brown, G. and Alexander, D. A, (2008) *Stronger Together: The 21st century case for Scotland and Britain,* Fabian Ideas 621, The Fabian Society, London

11 *The Scotsman*, 13 January 2008.

12 United States Declaration of Independence, in Congress, 4 July 1776

13 Proclamation signed by the Rhodesian government, 11 November 1965

14 Devine, T. M. (2006) *The Scottish Nation, 1700–2007*, London, Penguin

15 Ibid, pp.249–66

16 Ibid, p.252

17 Ibid, p.250

18 Ibid, p.257

19 Ibid, p.256

20 Ibid, p.258

21 Ibid, p.257

22 Porter, M. (1990) *The Competitive Advantage of Nations*, London, Macmillan

23 Ibid

24 See, for example, Danson, M. and G. Whittam (1998) Clustering, Innovations and Trust: the Essentials of a Clustering Strategy for Scotland, Working Paper, Department of Economics, University of Paisley; Botham, R. (1997) Inward investment and regional development; Scotland and the electronics industry. Paper to the Regional Science Association: British and Irish Section Conference, Falmouth

25 Bale K. and J. Lyons (2007) Fury As Sun Man Says Scots Sponge Off English, *Scottish Daily Record*, 13 Oct

26 Doyle, A. C. (1894) 'Silver Blaze', in *The Memoirs of Sherlock Holmes,* Gerge Newnes, London.

27 Forty-nine and half percent in Latin prelims. Fraserburgh Academy, 1963. I like to think there was a heritage and influence of Scottish engineering precision which led to that mark being awarded

28 See, for example, *Pattern in Corporate Evolution*, Oxford University Press, 2000.

29 See especially Davie, G. E (1999) *The Democratic Intellect: Scotland and Her Universities in the 19th Century*, Edinburgh, Edinburgh University Press; Paterson, L. (2003) *Scottish Education in the 20th Century*, Edinburgh, Edinburgh University Prsss

30 If you also have difficulty finding out who he is, that underlines my point.

31 Marine and Fisheries Agency (2007) *United Kingdom Sea Fisheries Statistics 2006*, Defra Publications

32 Evidence on GERS to Scottish Parliament Finance Committee, January 2007, Neil Kay

33 See Sachs, J. D and Warner A. (2001) 'The curse of natural resources' *European Economic Review* 45 827

34 Ibid

35 See: Regional Specialisation in the Long Run, Guy Michaels, October 2006 http://personal.lse.ac.uk/michaels/Michaels_ Specialization_Fall_2006.pdf,

Resource-Abundance and Economic Growth in the US Papyrakis, E. and Gerlagh, R. 2004 http://130.37.129.100/ivm/organisation/staff/papers/EER_resourcesUS.pdf

Does the Natural Resource Curse Apply to the United States? Cooke, C., Aadland, D. and Coupal R., May 2006 http://www.uwyo.edu/aadland/research/resourcecurse.pdf

36 *The Prince* by Nicolo Machiavelli Written *c.*1505, published 1515 Translated by W. K. Marriott for the Liberty Press

37 Casson, M. (1995) *Entrepreneurship and Business Culture, Studies in the Economics of Trust,* Vol.1 Edward Elgar, Aldershot, p.232

38 Quod erat demonstrandum p.74

CHAPTER 6

An English Voice in Scotland

BETTY DAVIES

This is the testimony of a prominent English businesswoman who has lived and worked in Scotland for over 40 years. Her varied career and experiences tempered by her long relationship with the leading Nationalist Douglas Henderson, led Betty Davies, finally, at the end of his life to accept Scottish Independence as the right way forward for the Scottish people. In this moving and challenging memoir, she explains why.

INSPIRED BY THE Edinburgh Festival and excited by the opportunities the country presented I came to work in Scotland after graduating from the Guildhall School of Music and Drama. Stepping off the overnight sleeper on an ice-cold February morning in 1963 and dragging a weighty suitcase to a waiting taxi, I emerged from Waverley Station to be stunned by one of the most dramatic skylines in Europe. The enlightened architects of Edinburgh had created a stage on which to play out the nation's history.

Now in the 'swinging '60s' of the 20th century change was in the air. Would I play a part in these changes? I was not to know that in the next 40 years an historic new drama would take place and that I would have a front seat in the stalls.

I had left behind in the Midlands of England security and family. I came knowing no one; but an introduction to the kindly Rev. Ian Simpson and his wife, whose daughter Myrtle was away mountaineering for a few weeks, allowed me to stay in her warm and comfortable room at the top of a graceful winding stair in the former home of Sir Walter Scott at 25 George Square. In this gracious historic house, I unpacked my suitcase and took stock.

As my first job was as PRO (Public Relations Officer) of the Scottish Gas Board, it was propitious that within days in post I learned that Sir Walter Scott had been first Chairman of the Edinburgh Gas Light and Coke Company. A few weeks later I began organising and mounting in the elegant drawing room a production of Pergolesi's opera, *La Serva Padrona*. It became a landmark event as the first artistic production to be sponsored by a nationalised industry during the Edinburgh Festival. I had made a start and the event provided a key that unlocked many doors and introduced me to the varied and colourful weft and warp of the fabric of Scottish life that would eventually change and define my perception and view of Scotland's relationship with England.

If variety is the spice of life, then perhaps my career can be described as lively. The foundation of the Edinburgh Theatre Workshop, the excitement of assisting in the early development of the Traverse Theatre and a stint at STV were natural extensions of my theatrical training. However, it was of course the enterprise of the Campus shops with the late Lorna Blackie that gave rein to my fashion sense and design skills, and prompted the development of Harris Tweed as a women's fashion fabric. Later the establishment of Scottish Fashion International and a client portfolio which included the branding of two Scottish banks and many major national institutions as well as formal robes for the choir of St Giles Cathedral, Napier University and Edinburgh College of Art. Now firmly established in Edinburgh and recognised as Scotland's leading designer, commissions followed to design for the first of Scotland's important women dignitaries – the Levee dress for the first Woman Herald of the Court of the Lord Lyon King of Arms, the formal dress for the first woman Moderator of the Church of Scotland and the first women High Constables of Edinburgh (tailed morning coats as worn by the gentlemen were hardly appropriate). Now as a consultant these varied and fascinating commissions gave me an insight to many aspects of Scottish life. It also engendered a deep love for a country which can only be acquired by living and working in it.

Illustrating the development of my career may indicate how immersed I was becoming in Scottish life. I also hoped that my experience would, in time, benefit others. As I journeyed from the Borders mills to the Outer Hebrides on the quest for unique fabrics and garment manufacturing to extend my design ranges to include more Scottish fabrics, it was obvious that many of the companies were struggling and facing closure. The weavers of Harris Tweed in their remote crofts were courteous to this strange Englishwoman who praised their skill, commissioned their work, while they feared for their livelihood and a way of life which was tough and relentless, but seemingly unhurried and timeless. Like the almost forgotten breed of the English hill farmers, their hands bear a legacy of the toil of generations and their heart the imprint of determination and survival.

Heading back to the mainland of Scotland, I could not escape the realisation that this land with its breathtaking landscape, immense natural wilderness, rich wildlife, diversity of language, laws and religion was unknown and unexplored by the majority of my own kinsmen. This was another country, as far from Westminster as Warsaw, and remote from the frenzy of the daily commute to a workplace that harnesses us to the desk, telephone and bench.

There were, of course, difficulties to surmount. A woman alone, and an Englishwoman working in a competitive environment, is particularly vulnerable. The barbs of the occasional xenophobic colleague hurt: 'Here two days and already you're empire building'. 'Your work is beautiful, but your voice is too English' was an unexpected comment from the BBC's Head of Radio, George Bruce, at my first audition. Was it worth staying here, I wondered? Years later, when inviting him to address an entranced audience at the RSA about his first meeting with the poet, Norman Soutar, I reminded him of our first encounter. 'It wouldn't happen now', he said. It does and it still hurts but now of course I have the security of a home, trusted friends and colleagues.

In those early days a hectic work schedule allowed little time for political distractions. As I travelled the length and breadth of Scotland,

I was unprepared for, and shocked by, the continuing high unemployment in Glasgow and by the abject poverty in many of the housing
schemes in the Central Belt. Coming from a thriving industrial city in
the Midlands of England, why, I wondered, was Scotland so attached
to Labour? Why were so many of the disaffected, the bitter and disillusioned blaming the English when they should be aiming their
verbal fire power at the negligence and complacency of their own
MPs? Surely there had to be a change?

Change came slowly and then gathered momentum. In November
1967, on the night we opened the Glasgow Campus shop, Winifred
Ewing, the charismatic Glasgow lawyer, won the Hamilton by-election.
Winnie, surrounded by hundreds of SNP supporters, boarded the train
for Westminster to put fear, not so much in the hearts of the English,
but in the loins of the Scots Labour MPs needed to shore up a failing
Labour Government. Change had arrived in the shape of an articulate,
attractive woman in a glamorous outfit and one of my hats.

During the period 1974–79, coincidental with the drama that was
being enacted in Westminster, my working life took me regularly to
London and with her renowned generosity, Winnie extended to me
the occasional use of her London flat. On frequent visits to the House
of Commons I was witnessing at close quarters the indefatigable
verbal assault that she and the band of seven SNP MPs elected in 1974
were inflicting on Callaghan's Government. They were relentless. An
articulate, feisty irritant group, like west coast Scottish midges – ever
present and a constant threat to the tribal instincts of diehard
Scottish Labour MPs at Westminster. These were heady days and in
the same year another election sent four more SNP Members to
Westminster.

Enter Douglas Henderson the SNP's indefatigable Chief Whip, the
Member for East Aberdeenshire, charged with delivering the strategic
negotiations to the other Parties with decisions hammered out during
the small hours that were to set the Labour Government into a frenzy
of wheeler dealing that might ensure its survival. Forever etched on
my memory is the sight of Douglas in action, a determined five foot

six inch dynamo setting off to the Whips' Office intent on achieving a successful outcome to his negotiations. It was a pivotal moment. This was history in the making as was the night on which he went through the Lobby to cast his vote following behind the Tory MP Michael Heseltine, and which, according to Tam Dalyell in his thoughtful obituary following Douglas's death, was the vote that brought down the Government. Douglas would have relished this epitaph.

As Douglas became more a constant presence in my life and career, his daily forensic analysis and commentary on political events inevitably extended my political education. I could hardly escape the conclusion that the present constitutional arrangements had to change if Scotland were to realise her cultural and economic potential. A committed Nationalist from the age of 14, holding all the high offices in the SNP with the exception of Chairman over a period of 50 years, Douglas gained the reputation, together with his university friend Gordon Wilson, as one of its most astute strategists. They both shared a burning zeal for Scottish Independence. Douglas deprecated a Devolved Parliament, concerned that it might present a long term acceptable alternative. After a long struggle with major surgery for cancer in the '90s which restricted his political activity he returned to the fray to fight for a seat in the European Parliament in 2004 and for Westminster in 2005. A whetted appetite to return to the cause for one last term, and the decision to stand for the Scottish Parliament in 2007 would have resulted in his serving as MSP in the present Scottish Government at Holyrood. Sadly this distinctive Scottish voice, and his energetic fight for Scotland's freedom, was silenced in September 2006 when he succumbed to pancreatic cancer. His untimely death robbed Scotland of one of its most effective politicians and one of the SNP's best orators. It robbed me of a gentle, generous-hearted and witty companion. The acceptance we shared for the love of our respected countries was never breached and during our long association my allegiance to responsibilities in England continued. Political discussion was often rather heated but on one question there was always total agreement, mutual love and pride in our distinctive heritage and cultures. During almost 30 years of an action-packed political and business relationship Douglas never once asked me where I cast my vote. It was an uncrossed boundary. In the last hours of his life he was harrowed by his failure to be able to continue to fight. It was then that I promised to take up his cause and vote SNP at the 2007 election.

Why was I able to make this decision was a question that my English friends often asked. It was because the ebb and flow of the changing interests of England and Scotland had dominated my political thinking for the past decade. I had watched with dismay the political ennui that engulfed and almost anaesthetised voters in England. So many things that in the past were regarded highly, the pillars on which love and pride in country were structured, were under threat and in danger of crumbling. When John Prescott was fighting to introduce another expensive tier of government, regional assemblies, in England, I feared that his objective was to emasculate further the collective voice of the country to create an even greater advantage to Labour.

In sharing with you the views that have influenced my thinking in relation to Scotland's future it is not possible for me to divorce my reasoning from the changes that have been wrought on England by the myopic, state controlled, cynical political philosophy of the last Labour government.

It was only during the last two years when Gordon Brown sensed that his mandate to govern might be in jeopardy that he saw the consequences of what his failure to face up to the criticism of what his pollsters on the doorsteps were telling him.

Realism and good sense led the electorate to deny any one of the major parties a clear mandate at the 2010 Westminster election. I have been aware for some time of a growing consciousness among my friends and acquaintances south of the border, that more than a fleeting thought is being given to the advantages and the consequences of separate Parliaments for England and Scotland. The legacy of this Labour Government is a deeply disillusioned electorate who now, in a time of economic uncertainty, no longer trust what politicians tell them. This is a very serious indictment of a government. In England there is increasing bitterness that unwelcome legislation has been passed because MPs from Scottish constituencies who, with the exception of the SNP Members, continue to vote on matters devolved to Scotland on which their own MSPs vote differently. This runs counter to common justice.

But perhaps the most damning and serious criticism is that of the contempt that has been shown towards the electorate by MPs of all Parties in the last Parliament who have used and abused their unique position and high office by indulging in expense claims that have betrayed the trust that has been vested in them. The dilemma of whom to vote for in the 2010 election, delivered a result that clearly demonstrated the confusion and mistrust that has given rise to a Coalition Government for the first time in over 60 years. We now have the sharing of responsibility by one near right of centre and one left of centre party led by two talented young leaders without former Cabinet responsibility. Television footage of two earnest young men embracing like long lost buddies gave hope that harmony would break out between the two parties for the common good; but already the untamed rump of the Liberal/ Labour faction could soon hinder progress just as the Liberal faction in the Scottish Government cosied up to Labour and totally hindered sensible progress and legislation for eight years. Now burdened with the legacy of Labour profligacy, the task ahead is daunting. The electorate can only hope that the early joint declaration of fairness, responsibility and freedom will hold fast for five years and that they will have the wisdom and courage to deliver what they promised to achieve.

Pride in country and the achievements of our ancestors are an essential part of what humanises and frees the spirit. It gives a light to the eye of the young that leads them to aspire to greater things and an awareness of what is possible. I believe that Cameron's charge to Brown that the last 13 years has led to a broken society has a great deal of truth in it. But that broken society has been more apparent in

England and my heart bleeds for some glaring omissions of misman-
agement and common sense. Conversely I have seen in Scotland,
despite the alarming collapse of the banks, a new sense of optimism
and confidence. Scotland with its five million inhabitants, since the rise
of Scottish Nationalism and the creation of its own Parliament, has
acquired a sense of greater stature and pride. The citizens of England
need the same opportunity.

As Gordon Brown dithered with his chronic uncertainty towards
the end of the last Parliament, David Cameron had the opportunity
to establish a credible alternative to Labour in England. He failed to
achieve a majority, and one of his failures may have been his lack of
understanding of the political temperature of the Scots. Perhaps he
has been inadequately informed. The terrier-like hold which Labour
has on the constituencies around Glasgow and the dominant left
wing allegiance of the Scottish press provides little hope of change.

Why is Labour in such serious disarray? Some of the rot set in
during the last years of the previous Government, although Gordon
Brown inherited from Chancellor Kenneth Clarke a reasonable economic situation which provided a pot of gold from which to go on a
spending spree. But its demise has been perpetuated and accelerated
by a New Labour administration which, mired in spin, seemed to
have lost sight of its ethical principles and the basic moralities of the
old Labour movement. The Labour administration, with all its good
intentions and high mindedness came into power intending to trans-
form Britain, only to spin out of control because of its inability to
manage the edifices it created.

In the early years of the new century here in Scotland we watched
with dismay as the devolved Government led by Labour with LibDem
assistance fumbled its way through eight years of being Westminster's
carpetbaggers. The Administration was in tatters. The opposition
SNP MSPs led by Alex Salmond, his Deputy Nicola Sturgeon and John
Swinney clearly stood head and shoulders above their Labour counterparts. If Labour in Scotland was to be deposed, we had at last been
offered a viable alternative. In 2007 I and many thousands of others

put our crosses for the first time in the box that produced the majority of one for the SNP, The significance of that vote will never be forgotten. Scotland had at last rejected the dead hand of Labour and now had an articulate, clever and industrious group of men and women who were given the opportunity to prove to the voters that they could and would work hard for the good of the country they so obviously loved. This dedication and pioneering spirit is still needed.

Before the result of the 2007 election was known I was walking down The Mound when Moira Salmond saw me and stopped the taxi in which she was driving – 'Betty' she said 'We've won. Alex has just left by helicopter to see the Queen. Wouldn't Douglas be pleased?' That he was not there to share the day was heartbreaking. What would he have done? He would have given a quiet smile of satisfaction and wept with joy. Scotland had at last led the way in ridding itself of a moribund Labour administration. Over the border three years later the former Iron Chancellor sadly metamorphosed into a crumbling Prime Minister and the electorate in England finally decided that they too had had enough. We observed with sadness and with some relief, a leading actor capable of a leading part on a world stage, but who on home ground seemed to be in the wrong theatre and in an unsuitable play. A good man with enormous strengths and gravitas who failed to win a mandate from the people is a personal tragedy of almost Olympian proportions. We all pay a heavy price for his failure.

The question now must be: Can the SNP continue to win another mandate? They have made a very good start. First Minister Alex Salmond has proved himself to be a real man o' the people and a formidable leader. Their Ministers are dedicated, intellectual, and competent in addressing challenging and changing issues. The forthcoming Scottish elections in 2011 promise a tough fight as Labour mounts an offensive to win back its stranglehold on its Labour heartland. It will no doubt try to re-invent itself as Labour now in opposition at Westminster also endeavours to do so. The SNP heralded a practical and refreshing new era of political thought which offers hope for the future of Scotland. At last, and only with a tiny majority, this was achieved. It now must be sustained not by an electorate immersed in the political shibboleths of the past but by an electorate that opens its eyes and looks to a future that does not rely on a Westminster Government burdened with the responsibility of acting responsibly for over 50 million people in a period of deep decline. I treasure the heritage of my country and understand why many of my fellow countrymen respect the monarchy, are proud of being British and regard Scotland highly – they want us still to be part of Britain – the romance of the country and its history is ingrained in many hearts and the severance of the Union is not something they want. But surely separate governance can be managed and ties strengthened by these proud nations treasuring and enhancing their strengths.

After the 2007 election Simon Jenkins wrote in *The Sunday Times*, welcome 'An autonomous Scotland, a country as big as Denmark, should liberate the English parliament to enjoy politics freed of the alien encumbrance of Scottish seats. It should liberate English politics, and especially the Labour party, from the distortion of 50 Scottish socialists, indelibly linked to old fashioned politics of public spending.' These are sentiments I share.

Douglas Henderson was right. The Labour administration under Prime Minister Callaghan, that Douglas helped to depose in 1979, believed that by embracing devolution Scotland would have a sleeping tiger that Labour could tame. Labour now realises, 30 years on, that the tiger is no longer sleeping and has woken to a new and brighter dawn.

Those who come to live in Scotland do so because they seek a better quality of life. They should embrace and support this country's heritage and its future. Three hundred years of the Act of Union is but a small step in the long, long history of these islands. We now live in a state that in the last 40 years has demographically altered beyond recognition. To treasure and develop our differing cultures and to meet challenging economic demands, not least from the emerging economies of Brazil, China and India, will inevitably require dramatic change.

We must move forward with courage, with confidence, and with goodwill. Above all we must accept the right of all the people in these islands to seek both good governance and self-determination.

Democratic Deficit

This chart shows the wholly different general electoral outcomes north and south of the Border, showing in sharp relief the political disunity of the 'United' Kingdom.

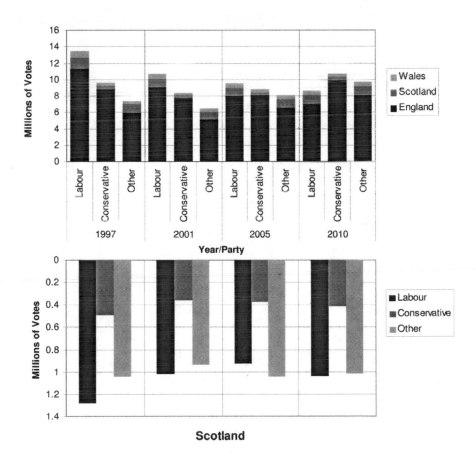

Postscript

Replies to people who have doubts about Scottish independence.

1. **Would the disentanglement of Scotland from the UK be a long and expensive process?**

   After Devolution we are already about half-way there. Even under the Union we retained many of our important institutions such as our legal system and important aspects of Scottish administration have been managed for years by the Scottish Office. Even without such advantages many long submerged European nations have recently become successful independent states without difficulty. There is no reason to suppose that there would be any particular problem in our own case

2. **The problems which mainly concern many people in Scotland are such matters as crime, street violence, addiction to drugs or alcohol, lack of jobs, rising costs, poor housing. Would independence help to solve them?**

   There are of course no magic cures, but small states do have an advantage in dealing with such problems. Their parliaments and governments are close to the people and can take decisions and act quickly. In the British state we are only about a 10th of the population and most attention, naturally and democratically, is given to the interests of the majority. Our problems may differ from theirs in nature or degree.

3. **An independent Scotland would need its own army, navy, air force and diplomatic service. Can we afford them?**

   We do not get such services at present without cost because part of the taxes which we pay in Scotland helps to finance them. They are therefore partly Scottish owned and we shall be entitled to a share on independence. Scotland would not then aspire, like

Britain, to the role of a nuclear-armed great power. Our own requirements would be much more modest and reasonable, similar to those of our small European neighbours such as Denmark. The cost might even be less than we at present contribute to the British establishment.

4   **Is Scotland too poor and too small to prosper with independence?**

Not in the least. As demonstrated in Independence is the Answer, the small independent countries in Europe are among the most prosperous in the world. Recent research by the National Science Foundation of the United States reached the conclusion that Denmark, which is smaller than Scotland in size and population, is the happiest of all countries. Our oil alone would make an independent Scotland very wealthy. It will not last for ever, but long enough to establish a capital fund as a guarantee of future prosperity. Scotland is rich too in other resources, fish, minerals, agriculture, and wind and tidal power. It has an educated and skilful population with a rich tradition in industry and scientific discovery.

5   **Is Scotland too small and too weak to survive in a potentially hostile world?**

It is not the small countries, but the larger ones with great power ambitions which are particularly vulnerable to military involvement. The British involvement in the disastrous Iraq war is an example. An independent Scotland, along with the other small countries of Europe, would not be a threat to others nor a provocation to terrorist attack.

6   **Would an independent Scotland be isolated in the world?**

On the contrary, independence would enable us to establish, or recover, our own direct relations with the rest of the world and enable us to become a member of international organisations such as the European Union and the United Nations.

7 **Would independence mean the end of our long association and friendship with England?**

Certainly not. We should both remain members of the European Union with free movement and free trade. There would be no barriers to the continuation of cross-border movements, friendships, and relationships of all kinds. In addition many of the tensions involved in the present devolution arrangements would be removed. This includes such problems as Scottish members of the Westminster Parliament being free to vote on policies which affect only England; and English suspicions (even if mistaken) that some of their taxes are used to subsidise Scotland. An independent Scotland as a member of international organisations such as the EU would be able to express and defend our own interests and points of view, but on many questions Scotland and England would be able to support one another. Our relations with England would be strengthened, not weakened, by the removal of the problems which disturb our present relationship.

8 **The SNP would have a political monopoly in an independent Scotland, which would ultimately lead to a one-party state. We'd lose all parliamentary debate and deliberation.**

It could be said that in an independent Scotland Labour could equally have a political monopoly, as the last devolved administration did for two terms. The monopoly by one party is extremely unlikely in an independent Scotland and members of an independent Scotland will not be in thrall to an English parliament in a way that the last Labour-led administration was.

The long crusade of the SNP is to achieve independence, not a super one party state of SNP representatives. What the SNP has been able to do is to convince the electorate that the one party state of Labour in Scotland for eight years has had its day. Labour has failed to recognise the need for greater opportunities and improved services for the Scottish people and to move with the times. The SNP interpreted the desire for change, and presented a convincing agenda of how to achieve it with many convincing policies. Within its membership, it has long been recognised that there are many people of different political colours from left, right and centre who will want to exercise these opinions when Scotland is independent. Their membership and allegiance for the SNP is because it is the only party with a dominating agenda for independence. When this is brought about – it is inevitable that these differentiating opinions will emerge.

Many people who voted for the SNP were not members of the party and if not members, were supporters of the other parties – Conservative, LibDem. Greens and SSP. As an independent parliament, there is likely to be keen competition from each political party for seats and high representation, this should result in a much healthier, virile and more democratic society.

9   **Going independent would reward the anti-English sentiment that already exists in Scotland. The thousands of English people living in Scotland (and the Scots living in England) would be forced to move.**

This is becoming an outmoded question and might be interpreted as emotive scaremongering. Unfortunately there remains some antipathy towards the English and it manifests itself unpleasantly in some areas. However we are living at a time where this is a great increase in mobility particularly by younger members of our society and racial, disrespectful comments are disliked and are treated with contempt.

Are we suggesting here that an independent Scotland would behave in a manner that would force the English to move? This cannot be – even the slightest slight whiff of something that smacks of even a veiled suggestion of 'ethnic cleansing would be unthinkable and totally abhorrent to the great majority of Scots.

If Scotland adopted a stance where it resented incomers, particularly the English, many of the fair-minded Scots and not the English would be amongst the first to leave.

Scots have integrated well in England for centuries, and their emphasis on good education, sense of family and thriftiness is respected. They also enjoy prominence in the news media and are noted as being good communicators.

As a Scottish government concentrates on improving education, social welfare and job prospects for all its citizens, even more opportunities and skills will be required. Already there is a marked increase in Scots returning to take up positions in Scotland again. There is a greater need for Scotland to welcome the talents that others bring. Insularity must be avoided at all costs.

10   **Within a few years, the Scottish electorate would revert to type and Scottish politics would be left/socialist/ Labour dominated for generations to the detriment of the Scottish economy – especially regarding inward investment.**

If Scotland reverted to type then it would be to the traditional open and internationalist perspective that characterised Scotland before the dull hand of the Union fostered defensiveness and negativity in some quarters.

11   **We'd need frontier posts all along the border.**

They do not need them between the EU countries that are members of the Schengen Agreement, there is no reason on earth why we would need them between Scotland and England. It would not be in the interests of Scotland or England.

12   **We'd be forced to join the Euro.**

It would be our choice whether or not to join the Euro, a choice in which we only have a minority voice just now.

13   I've no job, no prospect of one in the foreseeable future, my family can barely survive on benefits. What difference does it make whether we're governed from London or Edinburgh?

One of the advantages of a small state is that everyone in it is close to the centre of government. Problems encountered by people in Stornoway might seem remote to a government in London but they cannot be ignored by one in Edinburgh.